A Tale of Two Cities

This monograph has been awarded the Prize of
the Teylers Godgeleerd Genootschap.

J.A. LOADER

A Tale of Two Cities

Sodom and Gomorrah in the Old Testament,
early Jewish and early Christian Traditions

CONTRIBUTIONS TO BIBLICAL EXEGESIS AND THEOLOGY, 1

edited by Tj. Baarda and A.S. van der Woude

J. H. Kok Publishing House, Kampen

Mentem mortalia tangunt

In memory of Charles Dickens, whose tales of cities and people have always fascinated those who yearn for a healed and a loving and a just society

CIP-GEGEVENS KONINKLIJKE BIBLIOTHEEK, DEN HAAG

Loader, J.A.

A tale of two cities : Sodom and Gomorrah in the Old Testament, early Jewish and early Christian traditions / J.A. Loader. – Kampen : Kok. – (Contributions to biblical exegesis and theology : nr. 1)
ISBN 90-242-5333-0
SISO 226.3   UDC 22.07   NUGI 632
Trefw.: Sodom en Gomorrah.

© 1990, Publishing House J.H. Kok, Kampen, The Netherlands
Cover by Karel van Laar
ISBN: 90 242 5333 0
NUGI 632 – W boek

Preface

A Tale of Two Cities: with this monograph by J.A. loader a new series of biblical research is introduced to the scholarly world.

Its name, 'Contributions to Biblical Exegesis and Theology', specifies the group of scholars and interested readers at which this new series is aimed. The area of research is defined as biblical, which means that the series will include studies on the Hebrew Bible and the Greek New Testament. The series title may seem to confine the field of interest to exegesis and theology. To a certain extent this is true. The main goal of the series is to further the interpretation of the biblical writings and the study of the theological developments within the sacred scriptures of Judaism and early Christianity. Exegesis and theology are mentioned here in combination, not without reason, since they often tend to become two different disciplines. The editors, however, hope that the series may demonstrate that exegetical studies can contribute to our understanding of theological processes and vice versa.

Although the series title narrows the scope by the words 'biblical exegesis and theology', it does not a priori exclude other studies. The somewhat vaguer word 'contributions' has deliberately been chosen to make room for studies on other areas such as Qumran, Hellenistic Judaism, apocalyptic and intertestamental literature in general, as far as they contribute to biblical exegesis and theology.

The study by J.A. Loader on Genesis 18 and 19 is a good start to the new series. Methodologically it demonstrates research of high standing and original point of view, and it certainly makes a contribution to the area of research in biblical exegesis and theology. For the editors it came as no surprise that this monograph had been awarded the Prize of the Teylers Godgeleerd Genootschap. Therefore, it deserves to be published as the first volume of Contributions to Biblical Exegesis and Theology.

The Editors

Contents

1. INTRODUCTION   11

2. THE NARRATIVE OF GENESIS 18-19   15
   2.1. Three men visit Abraham (Gn 18:1-16)   17
   2.2. Abraham's question about Sodom (Gn 18:17-33)   26
   2.3. God's wrath over Sodom (Gn 19:1-26)   34
   2.4. Abraham witnesses the destruction (Gn 19:27-29)   43
   2.5. Lot and his daughters (Gn 19:30-38)   44
   2.6. Conclusions   46

3. SODOM AND GOMORRAH IN THE REST OF THE
OLD TESTAMENT   49
   3.1. The Book of Genesis   49
      Gn 10:19   49
      Gn 13:10.12.13   51
      Gn 14   53
   3.2. The other books of the Hebrew Old Testament   56
      Dt 29:22   56
      Dt 32:32   57
      Is 1:9.10   58
      Is 3:9   60
      Is 13:19   60
      Jr 23:14   61
      Jr 49:18, 50:40   61
      Ezk 16:44-58   62
      Am 4:11   65
      Zph 2:9   66
      Hs 11:8   67
      Lm 4:6   69
      Allusions to Sodom and Gomorrah   70
   3.3. Conclusions   72

4. SODOM AND GOMORRAH IN EARLY JEWISH
LITERATURE   75
   4.1. The Apocrypha   76

Ben Sira 16:7-10	76
SapSal 10:6-9	77
SapSal 19:13-17	79
3 Macc 2:5	80
4.2. The Pseudepigrapha	80
TLevi 14:6	80
TNaph 3:4, 4:1	81
TAsh 7:1	82
TBenj 9:1	82
TAbr 6:13	82
Jub 16:5-9	83
Jub 20:5-6	84
Jub 22:22, 36:10 84	84
SlavHen 10:4-6	85
ApEzr 2:19, 7:12	85
4.3. Philo of Alexandria	86
Abr 107-118, 119-132	87
Abr 133-146, 147-166	88
Abr 204-216, 217-224	90
Abr 225-235, 236-244	90
QuaestGn 4	91
PostC 175-177	93
MutNom 228, Sacr 122, Congr 109	93
ConfLing 27-28	94
Fug 121-122, 144, Ebr 164-166, LegAll 3:213	94
Som 1:85	95
LegAll 3:24, 197	95
Ebr 222-224, Som 2:191-192	95
4.4. Flavius Josephus	96
BJ 4:453	97
BJ 4:483-485	97
BJ 5:566	98
AJ 1:169-185	98
AJ 1:194-206	99
AJ 5:81	103
4.5. Rabbinic literature	104
BerR 41:3-10	104
BerR 42-43	105
BerR 48-49	106
BerR 50-51	108
Sanh 109a-b	111
4.6. Conclusions	116

5. SODOM AND GOMORRAH IN EARLY CHRISTIAN
   LITERATURE   118
   5.1. The New Testament   118
        Mt 10:15, Mk 6:11, Lk 10:12   118
        Lk 9:51-56   119
        Heb 13:2   120
        Mt 11:23.24   120
        Lk 17:22-37   120
        Rm 9:29   121
        Jude 7, 2 Pt 2:6   122
        Excursus: Sodom and Gomorrah in Qumran and
        the Samaritan community   124
        Rv 11:8   126
   5.2. Patristic literature   127
        Clement of Rome   127
        Justin Martyr   128
        Irenaeus of Lyon   128
        Clement of Alexandria   130
        Tertullian   130
        Pseudo-Tertullian   131
        Basil the Great   132
        Macarius of Egypt   133
        Jerome   133
        Eusebius   134
        Augustine   134
        A note on the Christian interpretation of the angels in
        Genesis 18   136
   5.3. Conclusions   138

POSTSCRIPT   139

WORKS CONSULTED   141

LIST OF ABBREVIATIONS   149

In this study the Harvard System of reference is used. However, when reference is made to a work of the commentary-type, the author's name only is used when it is obvious which page of the book is intended.

1. Introduction

In Jewish and Christian literature the cities of Sodom and Gomorrah, especially as they appear in the narratives of Genesis 18-19, are famous (or infamous) as symbols of wickedness. Statements to this effect can be found in many commentaries on Genesis and on those passages in the Old and New Testaments where mention of the cities is made. However, if one looks up the article 'Sodom und Gomorrha' in the standard reference work *Die Religion in Geschichte und Gegenwart* (Eissfeldt 1962:114-115), one finds only a few remarks about the destruction of the cities, the fact that this was ascribed to their wickedness, and the problem of whether the story is an etiology or a nebulous recollection of a pre-historic catastrophe. Most of the short article and its cited literature is about topography and archaeology and nothing is said about the tradition or its meaning 'in Geschichte und Gegenwart'. In the quarter of a century since the publication of this article the situation has not changed. A study of the biblical chapters of Genesis 18-19 has appeared recently (Rudin-O'Brasky 1982), but a systematic study of these traditions, their meaning, religious background and impact is still lacking. It is the purpose of the present investigation to provide in this need.

First of all, we shall have to define what we mean by the 'Sodom and Gomorrah traditions'. The obvious answer would be that this tradition exists of all those texts in early Jewish and early Christian literature where mention is made of either or both of the cities. Though such a general definition would not be wrong, it would be necessary to elaborate somewhat.

If we are to study the influence of the Sodom and Gomorrah traditions on later generations, that is, their impact as it can be determined in later texts, we are to begin at the fountainhead of the tradition. The most extensive biblical passage on Sodom and Gomorrah is the narrative of Genesis 18-19, and this text has – as part of the Holy Scripture of Jews and Christians – exerted considerable influence on those communities where its authority was accepted. It would, therefore, be quite legitimate to regard the narrative unit in Genesis 18-19 as the fountainhead and the later Jewish and Christian texts depending on it as the stream of the tradition. In this case we would be speaking of *one* tradition and we would be primarily interested in the *Wirkungsgeschichte* of Genesis 18-19. We will indeed be doing such an investigation in this book. However, our theme is a little more complicated than this. Our 'fountainhead' in Genesis 18-19 bears the marks of a stratified text, that is, a text in which evidence of earlier material can be detected. We therefore have a *prima facie* case that our fountainhead is not the earliest instance of the tradition. Moreover, it is possible in principle that the references to Sodom and Gomorrah elsewhere in the Old Testament, or some of them, are not dependent on Genesis 18-19, but on other lines of tradition. Then we will have different Sodom and Gomorrah traditions. It is also possible that such texts as well as Genesis 18-19 draw on the same source, in which case we will have one predominant tradition. In either case we may use the plural 'Sodom and Gomorrah traditions' since there are probably several traditions feeding a central one and clearly different branches can be identified at least in the later development of the Jewish and Christian traditions. In terms of our metaphor, we may say that a first reading of the relevant texts reveals the possibility that there are several arteries flowing underground, that these combine and become visible in the fountainhead appearing at Genesis 18-19 as well as in various other smaller fountains, and that this emanates in a stream which runs through early Jewish and Christian literature.

The logical starting point for our study is the extended narrative of Genesis 18-19. As I will argue below, these chapters form a cohesive narrative unit in which the episodes combine in a concentric way. Accordingly, our investigation will commence with an analysis of this structure in order to proceed to a description of the meaning of what we can appropriately call the 'Sodom Cycle'. Then we shall investigate the presence of earlier material in the narrative, in an endeavour to identify earlier arteries of the tradition stream.

The next stage will be a similar historical-critical study of the other references to Sodom and Gomorrah in the Old Testament. An endeavour will be made to determine their relation to our fountainhead in Genesis 18-19 and, if possible, to earlier traditions.

An important focal point of our investigation will be the Sodom and Gomorrah traditions in Jewish literature. The sheer volume of the literature in question calls for a limitation of what is to be incorporated in our study. A sensible cut-off point is the end of the Talmudic period, and we will therefore proceed until about 400 CE. Under 'Jewish literature' is subsumed, for our purpose, the Apocryphal and Pseudepigraphic literature, the works of Philo and Josephus, the Qumran literature, the vast body of Rabbinic literature, but also the midrashim contained in the Targumic versions of the relevant texts in Genesis, as well as Samaritan literature. Because of the nature of the targumim continual reference to them will be made in the appropriate places, while an excursus on the

Sodom and Gomorrah traditions in Qumran and the Samaritan community has for practical reasons been incorporated in Chapter 5 (after the discussion of the relevant New Testament texts, pp 124-126).

Our study will conclude with the Sodom and Gomorrah Traditions in the New Testament and early Christian literature. Here, again, we shall have to make a rather arbitrary caesura, and 'early Christian' will be interpreted to extend no later than about the fourth/fifth century. This makes sense because the line is drawn at Saint Augustine whose prominence ends an era that roughly coincides with the period of Jewish literature up to the Talmudic period.

The study of traditions and their impact is a historical enterprise, and therefore we will be using the tools of historical criticism. This does not mean, however, that the organisation of the text 'as it is', its patterns and structures are unimportant for our purpose. On the contrary, the only place where we can begin, is the text 'as it is', that is, the final form of the biblical text. In this regard we shall set ourselves the same task as Rudin-O'Brasky (1982) who also studied Genesis 18-19 by complementing a study of the structure of the text with a historical approach. We shall, however, at the same time try to avoid separating what should be two aspects of our method into two isolated approaches applied after each other, thereby divorcing the text 'as it is' and its underlying history (cf Gitay 1984:639-640 for a criticism of this aspect of Rudin-O'Brasky's work). Accordingly, an analysis of the structure of this text is the gateway both to the *Traditionsgeschichte* lying underneath it and to the *Wirkungsgeschichte* following it. This kind of close reading of the text 'as it is' yields information which could otherwise be overlooked, and will therefore also be an important aspect of our procedure.

We may now sum up the hypothesis from which our investigation will depart:

> *The Sodom and Gomorrah stories in Genesis 18-19 form a unit which inspired a rich tradition in early Jewish and Christian literature, but which also, together with other texts in the Old Testament, shows signs of the existence of earlier Sodom and Gomorrah traditions.*

We will set ourselves the task of testing this hypothesis and, in the event of its being corroborated, of determining as best we can what the traditions on both sides of the fountainhead looked like, what the dominant motifs in the various stages of development were, and in what relationships these motifs stood to their respective religious and philosophical contexts.

Prominence will be given to the discussion of *texts*, and the study will be arranged accordingly. In this way I shall endeavour to counteract the always present danger of the discussion of a preconceived *pattern* with the help of selected text-references.

2. The narrative of Genesis 18-19

Most commentators agree that we have a narrative unit extending from the beginning of Genesis 18 to the end of Genesis 19. Even Brueggemann (1982:162), who takes Genesis 18:1-15 as part of the previous section (Gn 16:1-18:15), speaks of Genesis 18:1-19:29 as one passage and of Genesis 19:30-38 as an appendix to the Sodom story. According to him the narrative of the three men visiting Abraham is 'loosely linked' to Genesis 18:16-19:38 by the device of the 'men'/'angels'/'messengers'. Although I concede that the passages about the visit of the men and about the daughters of Lot can be regarded as 'loosely linked' to the Sodom story because of their original independence, I also think that they are integrated more thoroughly in terms of their compositional function in the overall structure of Genesis 18-19. Westermann (1976a:60) also testifies to this situation by taking Genesis 18 and 19 together and at the same time bracketing the 'story of promise' in Genesis 18 with the previous three chapters as 'one group'. The compositional unity of Chapters 18 and 19 can be seen in an analysis of the structure of the passage. The organisation of the narrative can be presented as follows:

A 18:1-16 Three men visit Abraham
  B 18:17-33 Abraham's question about Sodom
    C 19:1-26 God's wrath over Sodom
            1-11 Two messengers visit Lot
            12-22 Rescue from Sodom
            23-26 Destruction of Sodom
  B¹ 19:27-29 Abraham witnesses the destruction
A¹ 19:30-38 Lot and his daughters

The symmetry of the narrative can be seen in various aspects of its structure:

First we may note that the narrative has a central section (C) in which a crescendo is developed. In this part the destruction story proper is set out in three scenes. Here we find a progression from the arrival of the messengers and their confrontation with the men of Sodom (vv 1-11) to the rescue of Lot and his family (vv 12-22) and then to the actual destruction of the city (vv 23-26). The progressive line in Section C is heightened by the mutually opposing elements of haste and retardation in its centre: Having several times heard the injunction to flee for their lives (vv 12,15), which has a tone of serious urgency, and having repeated it himself to his sons-in-law (v 14), Lot still hesitates (v 16). This creates tension, which is developed further by the urgent way in which the messengers physically compel Lot's family to leave, and by the command to hurry without even looking back (vv 16-17). The same forces of urgency and delay are employed in the ensuing conversation between Lot and God: On the one hand Lot finds time to request an alternative refuge and on the other God rushes him (*maher*) and makes the destruction dependent on the speed with which Lot can get away (vv 18-21).

An even more important observation is that the whole unit has a concentric structure. Working from the centre outwards, we find a Section B' that corresponds to Section B, and, on the outer sides, a Section A' that corresponds to Section A.

The inner circle, arranged as it is around the central section (C), serves to involve Abraham in the Sodom story. First, Abraham discusses the impending doom with God in a prelude to the destruction (Section B, 18:17-33), and, subsequent to the event itself, he looks at the aftermath of what has happened (Section B', 19:27-29). Encircled by 'prelude' and 'aftermath', the Sodom story is integrated into the Abraham story. Without having noticed the concentric structure, Gunkel (1910:xl) nevertheless observed a link between what I call Section B and Section B'. According to him the story-teller's keen insight in psychological processes made him link Genesis 18:20-21 (B) to 19:27-28 (B') – in the second passage Abraham satisfies his need to find out what the significance of the reference to Sodom's guilt in the first passage was.

The outer circle is marked by an antecedent in which three men visit Abraham and talk about his offspring (Section A, 18:1-16), and a postscript about Abraham's relatives and their offspring (Section A', 19:30-38).

The concentric pattern can be represented as follows:

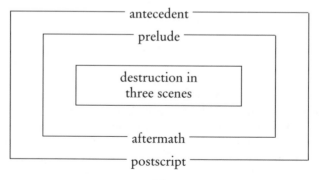

16

The concentric pattern can be represented This carefully planned pattern is consistent with the careful overarching composition of the Genesis/Pentateuch stories. The different sections are neatly sewn together at the seams. As the Primeval History (Gn 1-11) is interlocked with the Patriarchal History (Gn 12-50) by means of introducing Abraham in Genesis 11, and as the Patriarchal History in turn is dovetailed into the Exodus Story (Ex 1-15) by the overlapping features of the figure of Jacob and the locality of Egypt, so the sections of what we may safely call the 'Sodom Cycle' (cf the concentric or 'cyclic' pattern!) are also welded together: The visit to Abraham by the three men (Section A) prepares for the discussion about Sodom between Abraham and one of them (Section B), whereas the other two, who leave for Sodom, can be identified with the messengers who arrive in Sodom (Section C) (cf Gn 18:16.17.22; 19:1). Moreover, the dialogue in Section B about the impending destruction naturally leads to the account of the destruction itself in Section C whereas Abraham's observing the devastation (Section B') naturally follows it. Finally, the episode about Lot's daughters and their offspring (Section A') is a direct result of the catastrophe.

Whatever we may later decide about the date of the author of this story and whatever we may conclude about the earlier form(s) of the tradition(s) found in our narrative, we may on the grounds of our analysis so far concur with Van Seters's obvious regard for the 'highly literate' abilities of the author (Van Seters 1975:210), and with the admiration of commentators from Dillmann and Gunkel to Von Rad and Westermann for the artistry evident in the narrative.

2.1. Three men visit Abraham (Gn 18:1-16)

The end of this passage is given as verse 16 by some commentators (e g Procksch and Von Rad), while others take the caesura to be at the end of verse 15 (e g Skinner and Brueggeman) and yet others find it in the middle of verse 16 (e g Gunkel and Westermann). While something could be said for each of these demarcations, the former has more in its favour than the other two. This is so not only because the reader feels a 'sense of ending' brought about by the prehistory of the material (Von Rad), but also because of the use of pronouns in verses 16 and 17. The third person masculine plural in *wayyašqipû*, *'immâm*, and in *lᵉšallᵉḥâm* clearly refer to *hā'ᵃnāšîm* in the first half of the verse, which is a binding factor and militates against a division at verse 16a. On the other hand verse 17 begins with a new subject which takes up the first position in the sentence. The names of Yahweh and Abraham are explicitly mentioned instead of pronouns, and this makes for a new beginning.

The passage is neatly built up:

A. Introductory statement (v 1)
B. Arrival of the visitors (v 2)
C. Abraham's hospitality
   i) Invitation (vv 3-5)
   ii) Meal (vv 6-8)
D. Conversation after the meal
   i) Promise (vv 9-10)
   ii) Parenthesis (v 11)
   iii) Sarah's laugh (vv 12-15)
E. Departure of the visitors (v 16)

Sections A and E (arrival and departure) form a kind of *inclusio* and therefore corroborate our demarcation of the unit.

Verse 1. The story begins by explaining the visit of the men as a divine appearance to Abraham. The opening words supply us with the necessary setting for what is to follow and interpret the visit of the three men as a visit by Yahweh. The events themselves are described from verse 2 onwards, and therefore the introduction consists only of verse 1 and not, as Westermann maintains, of verses 1-8, which amounts to half the passage. Westermann is right, however, in observing that the verse is later than the original story, not only because of the mentioning of Yahweh but also because of the fact that Abraham is *not* mentioned. This can only be understood from the perspective of the compiler of the overall Abraham cycle. Kilian's reconstruction which supplies *'abrâhâm* for *hû'* (Kilian 1966:97, 187) remains a guess, albeit a probable one (cf Van Seters 1975:210).

Verse 2. When Abraham looks up, he suddenly realises that three men have arrived. 'So überraschend tritt Göttliches immer auf' (Gunkel; cf Gn 21:19, 22:13, Ex 3:2, Jos 5:13). The introductory statement has made the reader aware of the probability that their visit has something to do with Yahweh, but it does not suggest that Abraham also was aware of such a probability. Such a suspicion would have spoiled his genuine hospitality towards tired wayfarers. His haste to greet them and his courteous manner only show him to be true to the sacred duty of hospitality (cf Gn 19:2-3, Jdg 19:20-21; cf also Skinner 1930:299). Here we are already confronted by the dominant aspect of the *Traditionsgeschichte* of Genesis 18-19, notably the relationship between 'the men' in these chapters and Yahweh. Although Westermann finds no line of suspense ('Spannung') in the narrative, it is obvious that a certain expectation has already been created after only two verses. Is Yahweh among the three men? Are they his messengers? Or is he perhaps somehow present in all of them? These questions are awakened by the mentioning of the appearance of Yahweh and of the three men in almost the same breath. Whatever we shall find after having later considered the problem in more detail, *the relationship between Yahweh and the men has already assumed a positive literary function at the beginning of the story*. Whatever may have been early and whatever may have been later and whoever may have been responsible for the different stages, we can already see that the 'singular' and the 'plural' perspectives have not been merely conflated naïvely to form a badly polished narrative with the scars of its history carelessly left untended. On the contrary, the mentioning of the appearance of Yahweh and of the three men has stimulated our interest to read further. We shall have to attend to this phenomenon carefully (cf Gitay 1984:639, who mentions in his criticism of Rudin-O'Brasky her lack of interest in this issue).

Verses 3-5. The singular/plural issue is prominent in the next subsection. In verses 3-5a Abraham extends his courteous invitation and in verse 5b the men answer. Abraham's part in the little dialogue contains three pronominal elements in the second person masculine singular and eight in the second person masculine plural. This may be read in different ways. In the light of what follows, it could be interpreted that one of the men is the leader (Procksch) or that this one is Yahweh (Dillmann, Scharbert); it could be taken to mean that Yahweh is equally represented by all three men (Delitzsch; not Skinner as claimed by Procksch); we could regard it as an unevenness and opt for different sources, one 'singular' and one 'plural' (Kilian 1966:98-99); it would also be possible to explain the oscillation by the thesis of the combination of two different versions of the story (Westermann). Depending on which option is exercised, a decision about the pointing of the word *ʾadonay* can be made. Written with *pataḥ* it would mean 'Sirs', with *ḥîrèq* it would mean 'Sir', and with *qâmèṣ* it would mean 'Lord'. The present pointing is obviously intended to square Abraham's words with verse 1 (Zimmerli), but the form with *pataḥ* can also *sound* ambiguous ('Sirs' and 'Lord') which would suit the oscillation of the singular and the plural: We have three men, but one of them may be God. Although Von Rad reads *ʾadonî*, he sees a suggestive double meaning ('Doppelsinn') in the fact that Abraham is thought of as 'finding favour in your (singular) eyes': This is only an expression of courtesy, but it also suggests Yahweh's favour. If that is so, then it could also be said that the whole dialogue with its simultaneous use of singular and plural reflects such a 'Doppelsinn'. Why could the story-teller, whether he was a redactor or compiler or a receiver of traditions, not have created such an ambiguity? Even if we have before us the result of the conflation of two earlier forms of the story, there is no reason to regard the evidence of the combination as devoid of positive literary effect. Cf Van Seters 1975:155, who makes the valid point that the conflation of several versions 'that are only partially utilized in the final version' is in fact 'an act of composing a narrative' and not just 'editorial procedure'. Brueggemann 1982:157-158 ascribes a heightening effect to the vacillation of identity. Vawter 1977:226 detects an intended ironical twist in the matter. Speiser regards it as a literary effect that makes the reader 'share Abraham's uncertainty'.

Verses 6-8. Here the meal, or rather, the preparation for the meal is described. Westermann has seen that liveliness is brought into the story by the description of Abraham's haste in getting the meal prepared instead of a mere enumeration of the menu. This is indeed so, but there is also a remarkable similarity in structure between this subsection and the previous one. In both cases an elaborate report is given of what Abraham says/does, and in both cases an almost abrupt statement is made on what the men say/do (respectively vv 3-5a/6-8c and vv 5b/8d). This tallies with their sudden appearance (v 2) and adds to the mysterious aura surrounding the men. Not only is Abraham contrasted with the men (verbosity and detail against brevity), but the degree of suspense is also heightened (cf Westermann's view that there is no suspense in the story, and Brueggemann 1982:157, who claims the opposite): The short sentences of verses 6-8 match the hurry with which Abraham runs about and rushes his wife and slave, thereby creating an expectation in the reader. But Abraham's speed is counteracted by the copious information provided at the same time, which slows down the pace at which the story moves. The two forces of haste and retardation work against each other and therebycreate tension. We can also relate these narrative techniques to the symmetrical composition of the subsection: The opening sentences of verses 6 and 7 are organised chiastically (verb + Abraham, direction; direction, verb + Abraham) and as such flank a sentence about Sarah's hurried contribution to the preparations; following this, a sentence about the slave's hurried contribution to the preparations is flanked by two sentences with identical openings (*wayyiqqaḥ, wayyittèn* in v 7b,c and again *wayyiqqaḥ, wayyittèn* in v 8a,b). This is careful storytelling.

Verses 9-10. Having eaten while being waited upon by their host (v 8c,d), the men begin their conversation. Their question involves Sarah and rouses more interest within the reader because it introduces a new element. Surely something is to emanate from the generous way in which Abraham has treated his remarkable guests? Would Sarah have anything to do with it? Again the storyteller exploits ambiguity and suggestiveness. On one hand he has the men (plural) commence the discussion and on the other he has one of them (singular) continue as if the singular pronominal element in *wayyô'mèr* (v 10) is identical to the third person plural in *wayyô'm'rû* (v 9) (cf Van Seters 1975:210-211). This is no more an inattentiveness than the implication of the question, namely that the men/man are ignorant of Sarah's whereabouts even though they know her name. It is neither said how they knew this nor that Abraham found it extraordinary. His answer shows that the men could neither see nor hear Sarah (Von Rad), which becomes important in verse 13 where Yahweh knows that Sarah has laughed notwithstanding her seclusion. The introduction of Sarah was not without reason, for now we learn that Abraham will indeed be rewarded for his hospitality and that Sarah will indeed be involved – she will give him a son. The 'Gastgeschenk' (Gunkel) is unusual in that it is a human being and in that it can be given only by a divine being. Sarah listens from behind the tent-door while the speaker has his back to it and can therefore not see her. This is quite natural (cf Skinner) and is not presented as evesdropping. The fact that she is amused by what she hears, must have a good reason because it overrides the surprise that she should have felt at a stranger's knowledge of her name. Commentators usually say that the speaker also reveals his knowledge of Sarah's childlessness, which is wrong, for the promise of a son does not imply that the receiver does not already have one.

Verse 11. Westermann takes the parenthesis to be an appended description of the 'Ausgangssituation' (childlessness) which should have been given at the beginning. In fact it does not mention childlessness at all. It may be normal for stories like this to provide such information at the outset, but in this case the reader already knows about 'the great blank' in Abraham's and Sarah's life (Skinner). The fact that we have an old story in a new compositional context does not allow us to merely assume that the 'Ausgangssituation' has become clumsy by being moved to its new position. It serves a useful purpose at this point and is not a disturbance of the narrative as Westermann thinks. Sarah's amusement (v 12) is substantiated by the explanation (v 11) that biologically she *cannot* have children any more, not that she *has* no children. Therefore the parenthesis enhances the wonder of the gift (v 10) and simultaneously leads to the next section.

Verses 12-15. Sarah does the natural thing for an old woman who overhears the words of verse 10 – she laughs by herself (*b^eqirbâh*). Speiser's idea that this is an 'impetuous reaction' and implies derision, ignores the importance of verse 11. This is followed by what we may call a trialogue. Yahweh addresses Abraham, but Sarah is the one who comes out and answers. She answers because of fear. This explanation, a 'psychologism' typical of the Jahwist (Von Rad), is given in a little parenthesis (v 15b) which links the statement of Sarah's denial (v 15a) and its rejection by Yahweh (v 15c) in the same way as the linking of verses 9-10 and 12-15 by the explanatory parenthesis in verse 11. It is now obvious even to Sarah that a man who can sense that she has laughed behind his back is remarkable (which does not, as Van Seters 1975:211 claims, amount to a 'moment of recognition', for to fear in such circumstances is quite natural). Therefore she lies in her own defence. Once again it is an understandable thing to do for a woman who had innocently and unsuspectingly (cf Gunkel) smiled at a wayfarer's reference to herself. This is respected by Yahweh who does unmask her laughter and her lie, but does not rebuke or punish her. Again we see an ambiguity: On one side Sarah has all the reason in the world to chuckle at the thought of sexual pleasure and the birth of a son for two old people. On the other, there is something strange about the man who has made the promise – no one, least of all a woman, dares laugh at the promise of a man who knows things no ordinary human can know. The climax of the issue is stated in the rhetorical question *hᵃyyippâlê' miyyahwèh dâbâr* (v 14). The fact that Yahweh speaks of himself as 'Yahweh' adds sonority to a statement of principle (all the analogous examples advanced by Gunkel concern messengers of Yahweh who refer to him, whereas the subject here is simply *yahwèh*; cf Gn 18:17-19). The gift is to be something wonderful, befitting the God who can do anything – an idea that has already been prepared by the parenthesis in verse 11. Its importance is indicated by the repetition of the promise. We do not hear of any return to Sarah later on, which indicates that the original ending of the story has been replaced by Genesis 21:1-7, where we hear of the fulfilment of the promise and the naming of the son, *yiṣḥâq*, in an obvious allusion to Sarah's laugh (*ṣḥq*, Gn 21:6).

Verse 16. The passage ends with the departure of the men, as it began with their arrival. Not only Yahweh, but all three of them turn towards Sodom. Abraham fulfils the last obligation of ancient near eastern hospitality by accompanying them. This brings the theme of his hospitality to a fitting close, but it is also necessary to make the following scene possible (Abraham's conversation with Yahweh, Gn 16:17-33). The verse functions as an ending to the story of the visit, as a link with the following conversation about Yahweh's righteousness, and as a preparation for the story of the destruction of Sodom (cf Gn 18:22, 19:1). It is a stepping stone in that it ends one scene and simultaneously effects continuation with another. The complex of related events or 'Ereigniszusammenhang' spoken of by Von Rad thus entails both the story of the promise *and* the Sodom story.

As far as the prehistory of the passage is concerned, we may now consider the direction in which the evidence points. We have found evidence of the presence of earlier stages in the story. The clearest instance is God's promise to return (vv 10, 14), which is not fulfilled and is supplanted by another ending (Gn 21:1-7). However the most disputed pointer to the

22

presence of earlier traditions is the fact that the visitors are referred to both in the plural and in the singular, suggesting a polytheistic and a monotheistic perspective. This in turn suggests an early or pre-Yahwistic version in which it was possible to have three gods visit humans, and a later version in which the Yahwistic monotheism is found. The tendency of the evidence is clear: There have been earlier strata in the tradition. The controversial point is how to interpret this. This problem has been tackled in various ways.

The simplest 'solution' is that proposed by E.I. Fripp almost a century ago, namely to assume one original story according to which only Yahweh visited Abraham (Fripp 1892:23-29). This means that the text has to be 'emended' extensively in order to remove the references to visitors in the plural and thus make the hypothesis tenable. For that reason alone this option should be rejected, not to mention its unsubstantiated assumption that a polytheistic version could not have existed.

Directly opposed to this is the thesis of two originally separate sources, a 'plural source' and a 'singular source'. This was advanced by Kraetschmar in conscious opposition to Fripp (Kraetschmar 1897:81-92) and has been revived again in a detailed argument by Kilian (1966:96-111, 148-160). Kilian painstakingly separates the two sources and assigns the following to his plural source: Verses 1b*, 2*, 3*, 4, 5, 7, 8, 9aα, 16; for the rest of the chapter: 20-21 (as words of the three men), 22a. The following is assigned to his singular source: Verses 1b (edited from the plural source), 2*, 3b*, 6*, 9aβb, 10-15; for the rest of the chapter: 17, 18, 20-21 (as edited version of the plural source), 22b, 23-33 (Kilian 1966:110-111). He has to submit that various additions, subtractions and overlappings occur (indicated by the asterisks), which, to say the least, does not contribute to the clarity of the thesis (cf Van Seters 1975:211, who points out the completely fragmented nature of the sources and Kilian's unconcern about it). This means that one of Kilian's sources has to be envisaged as a reworking of the other. The author of the later source has to be seen as the editor of the earlier one. Kilian calls his two sources 'zwei grosse Schichten' (1966:110) and 'zwei Großschichten' (1966:182). However, the singular source, which according to him is Yahwistic, exists by virtue of reworking the pre-Yahwistic plural source. It is an 'Ueberarbeitung' (Kilian's own word) of the earlier source. What, then, is the essential difference between this thesis and Gunkel's solution of 'Ueberarbeitung' which Kilian explicitly rejects (1966:182)? Do we have two sources as Kilian claims all along or one reworked source as his argument asserts? It seems to me that this source division falls short of producing the result for which the whole enterprise of 'Quellenscheidung' is designed, notably the isolation and identification of source documents. If one of the two supposed sources is only a redactional layer, it is not a source at all and it becomes impossible to distinguish between *Literarkritik* and *Redaktionskritik*.

Van Seters is quite severe in his criticism of Kilian (cf 1975:210n, 211n, 217n and especially 219n where he describes some of Kilian's notions as 'complete nonsense' with 'no scientific support whatever'). He brings a salutary perspective into the debate, which, however, also has its dubious aspect. According to him we should take seriously the *dependence* of sources on one another instead of assuming their independence (1975:157). Applied to Genesis 18 this would mean that an 'older story', in which the gods visited humans (and subsequently destroyed 'a certain place'), was reworked with considerable freedom by an Israelite 'author in a highly literate period' (Van Seters 1975:210). A measure of rhetoric is contained in this formulation for it suggests that 'highly literate' activity should be associated with a late date, which is, of course, germane to Van Seters's overall thesis. The welcome effect of all this is that it dampens overenthusiasm for reconstructing sources and traditions as if it were our only task to construe possible pictures of what the oldest strata underlying our text could have looked like *without due regard for the sense made by the final text*. On the other hand, however, Van Seters goes too far in belittling all efforts to reconstruct traditions underlying our present text. According to him the theme of the 'heavenly visitors', which is found often and in various cultures (cf the overview given by Gunkel 1910:193-194), is not a literary genre with a fixed form (1975:209) and if the actual, fixed form of a tradition cannot be demonstrated, 'one has said nothing at all' (1975:157). But if evidence within a text points to the use of earlier traditions in it, it does make sense to hypothetically reconstruct such earlier forms in order to *explain those traits in the text*, which is not just 'wishful thinking' about '*the* pre-Israelite history' of such a theme (cf Van Seters, 1975:210). Why should we know the form of a tradition before the hypothesis of such an earlier tradition can be helpful? Does the hypothesis of murder only make sense if it is already known who the murderer is and what he looks like? Hypothetical reconstructions can be very helpful tools. So Van Seters's idea of an Israelite author who used a non-Israelite (not necessarily pre-Israelite) story about gods visiting humans 'to fill out a purely Israelite tradition about divine destruction of Sodom and Gomorrah' is not far from what I would like to suggest, but it is accompanied by a dubious view of the reconstruction of traditions.

The principle that I have just defended is applied by Westermann. He takes no flights of fancy into the history of our passage, but advances an explanation of characteristics of the text in need of elucidation. Some of these characteristics which impress him as problematic (like the so-called long introduction and awkward position of the 'Ausgangssituation') are not problems at all and have been discussed above. However, the oscillation of plural and singular in the text does call for adequate clarification. Westermann offers the theory of a conflation of two independent stories as such an explanation. He even says what the structure of each was. The one (called 'A') was structured: childlessness as distress – announcement of the elimination of the distress. The other (called 'B') was structured: divine visit – hospitality – promise of a child as gift. These are actually found, respectively in a Ugaritic text (Krt I/1-58) and in Ovid (Fasti 5:494ff). The interchange between plural and singular is therefore to be attributed to the fact that one of the stories (presumably B) concentrated more on the visit by three men, while the other story (presumably A) focussed on the promise of one messenger. On these grounds Westermann rejects both Kilian's source division and Gunkel's solution of 'Ueberarbeitung' as 'unnecessary'. Having already dealt with Kilian's views, the first question that we can put to Westermann is what makes his own hypothesis more necessary than Gunkel's. The main obstacle is that he too assumes that whoever put the two stories together merely superimposed the one onto the other and left the scars of illogical and arbitrary alternation ('willkürliche Wechsel') lying there. Could the compositor not have meant something by alternating plural and singular? Couldn't he have been at work on composing his own literary text while *using*, not merely *compounding*, older stories? Can the alternation not have a positive literary effect? The necessity for this kind of question has caused much of the disillusionment with the traditional historical criticism from within the historical school itself and from the side of the so-called 'literary' approaches to the text. Moreover, Westermann's two original stories themselves seem problematical. Our narrative as we have it fits his Story B precisely so that no Story A is necessary. Westermann's Structure A would only have meaning for Genesis 18:1-16 if specific mention were made of childlessness as distress at the beginning (Westermann's 'Ausgangssituation'), which is not the case. So this whole thesis, while built on the sound basis of searching for earlier material as explanation for the present state of the text, also falls short of offering a convincing solution to the problem.

If neither a conflation theory nor a source division is acceptable, then we are left with another possibility – the reworking ('Ueberarbeitung') by one author of older material. In my discussion of the various sections of the passage I have argued that the narrative is carefully structured and that it carries evidence of literary sensitiveness. The use of both the plural and the singular where Yahweh is concerned creates an ambiguous effect and the narrator of our passage is to be *credited* with a skilful handling of the material he had at hand.

In the light of the widespread theme of the divine visit and the suggestion of a polytheistic presence among humans, we may accept that the earlier story was about three gods who visited a childless but hospitable man. Theoretically this story may have been Israelite, but 'So etwas ist mit Israels Glauben unvereinbar', says Kilian (1966:149). Although this remark is open to debate, he is to be agreed with when he opts for a non-Israelite origin, because a polytheistic Israelite story is less likely than a polytheistic story of non-Israelite origin. Procksch takes this position in his commentary (1913:112) where he calls the earlier story 'foreign material', and in his earlier monograph (1906:340-341) where he calls it 'Canaanite'. In the latter context Procksch says: 'Die mythologische Hülse einer Mehrheit himmlischer Wesen ist so geistreich und glücklich ... mit monotheistischem Inhalt erfüllt'. I believe this is what my analysis above has made acceptable. Not only has an early non-Israelite tradition been taken over in Israel (cf Vawter 1977:226), but it has been done successfully. Both the nebulosity in which the reader is kept about whether/when Abraham recognised Yahweh, and the plural/singular issue shroud Yahweh in mystery and successfully integrate foreign material into a Yahwistic context.

This foreign story has very old characteristics (like the eating god, reclining at the meal and the absence of wine, cf Gunkel 1910:200) and must therefore not only be non-Israelite, but also pre-Israelite. It has been taken over by Israel and associated with Mamre-Hebron and Abraham. The storyteller who so skilfully handled the plural/singular issue, that is, the problem of moulding a polytheistic story into a monotheistic story, was the one who moulded the non-Israelite story into the narrative we have (cf the criticism of Rudin-O'Brasky by Gitay, 1984:639, in his review of her book).

2.2. Abraham's question about Sodom (Gn 18:17-33)

Having already determined the beginning of this passage, there is little difficulty with its demarcation at the end of the chapter. In Genesis 19:1 the men seem leaving Abraham's tent (Gn 18:16) and going to Sodom (Gn 18:22), arrive in the city where Lot sits at the gate. With the new scene and the new company starts a new passage. Like the first, the second passage is neatly structured:
A. Introduction (vv 17-19)
B. Conversation
   i) Opening statement (vv 20-21)
   ii) Parenthesis (vv 22-23a)
   iii) Dialogue (vv 23b-32)
C. Departure (v 33)

There is some similarity in the structure of Genesis 18:1-16 and 17-33. Both passages contain a section in dialogue form, both have a parenthesis in the course of the conversation, and both end with a departure scene. It is often claimed that the passage has a reflective character (cf Gunkel, Von Rad, Westermann, Van Seters 1975:212 and others). Although this is true, it does not mean that the passage should not be read as a story. Our passage is presented as a narrative, as part of a story which *tells* something and not as a reflexion (which is found, for instance, in the Book of Ecclesiastes). If we distinguish, as we should, between textual organisation and textual function, we find that our passage is organised according to the conventions of narration, but that it functions as an argument for a certain proposition.

Verses 17-19. Yahweh is pictured as speaking to himself and in verse 19 he refers to himself in the third person singular. This does not mean, as Procksch and Schmidt (1976:134-135; cf Noth 1948:259n) maintain, that verse 19 is a later addition, for the same happens in verse 14 (cf above) where nothing of the sort is at issue. Neither do the substantiations for God's revelation to Abraham offered in verses 18 and 19 exclude one another as Schmidt (1976:135-136) thinks. The promise of becoming a great nation (v 18) and the necessity of being an obedient nation (v 19) exclude each other neither logically nor in terms of the tradition history of the patriarchal narratives (because the formulas connected with the motif of the great nation became fixed and could therefore be associated with the obedience motif – cf Westermann). God's reasons for telling Abraham what his plans are (*^{a}nî 'ośè* in v 17 is a *futurum instans*), are given in this section. Various aspects stand out in this regard. **First**, mention is made of Abraham's position as the father of the nation through which all the other nations (twice *gôy*) will be blessed. This has profound effect in the context, for the fate of one of these *gôyîm*, Sodom, is now at stake and Abraham is, as it were, compelled by his title of father of the blessed nations (cf Gn 12:3) to raise the issue of Sodom's fate. **Second**, he should be informed about Sodom's lot because he is to command his descendants to 'keep the way of Yahweh' (the parallel expression 'to do *ṣ^{e}dâqâ umišpâṭ*' is usually found in the opposite order, viz *mišpâṭ uṣ^{e}dâqâ* – Delitzsch). Therefore Sodom becomes an exemplary case which illustrates what happens to a nation who is wicked. If this people take this to heart, it will be possible for Yahweh to fulfil his promises to them instead of punishing them. This perspective, too, has a literary function in that it shows a form of piety which needs that kind of vindication of its faith in God's justice at issue in verses 23b-33. Here we see that the promises of Yahweh are not regarded as unconditional, but linked to the obedience of the receivers. This is not

27

necessarily a sign of a post-exilic date for the passage (which also goes for the word-order at the beginning of the sentence, where the consecutive form is avoided). **Third,** an interesting word is used to indicate reverence for Abraham's merit. He is the only one 'known' by God; we would expect the verb 'choose' (*bḥr*), but the curious use of *yd'* attracts the reader's attention. It is the same word used in Genesis 19:5 for the aggression of the Sodomites (Brueggemann). The motif of Abraham's uniqueness is not only confined to the opening verses of the passage, but also has a meaningful literary effect: Only a human being of such stature can dare to converse with God in the way that Abraham is about to in the following verses.

Verses 20-21. These verses can be read in various ways. They can be taken as words addressed to Abraham (which I have done, cf the sketch of the structure above). But it is also possible to take them as a self-addressed speech by Yahweh. In both cases it is obvious that we here have an older introduction to the Sodom narrative proper (cf the introductory formula with consecutive *waw* as opposed to the *waw* with perfect in v 17). In verses 17-19 Yahweh has already made up his mind what to do to Sodom and uses the ingressive form *'ᵃnî 'ośè*, but in verses 20-21 he still has to find out whether things in Sodom and Gommorah are really as bad as the rumours about the cities claim (*zᵉ'āqâ* suggests complaints that violence or injustice has been done, cf Hab 1:2). However this is not just a clumsy juxtaposition of two mutually excluding introductions. The second, older, one serves a useful literary purpose in helping to isolate Yahweh from his two companions and to get rid of them. What is needed for the purpose of the present passage, is that Yahweh alone remains with Abraham on the road along which Abraham had accompanied the men (v 16). By saying that he wants to know what is going on in Sodom and Gomorrah Yahweh in effect sends the two men off so that this can be achieved. Though this is not what Dillmann says, he has seen that verses 20-21 connect the following conversation to the previous verses. Therefore Skinner is wrong in reprimanding him for this insight.

Verses 22-23a. These verses are parenthetical in two respects: They divide Yahweh's initial words from the conversation starting at verse 23b, and they separate the three men. It is only now possible to see clearly that one of the men who had visited Abraham's tent was Yahweh. Verse 22 could have followed directly on verse 16, in which case Yahweh would have gone to Sodom personally. It is quite possible, and indeed probable, that the earlier, non-Israelite, story told how the deity went there himself (cf Wellhausen 1889:27-28, Gunkel, Skinner). In this regard Westermann is to be agreed with when he calls verse 22 an 'Uebergang' (cf Rudin-O'Brasky), but not when he judges the dovetailing of different sections to be jerky. The later author has arranged the available material in such a way that the scene is set for his theological discourse in dialogue form, and also that the two men who arrive in Sodom according to Genesis 19:1, prove to have been messengers all along. In other words, he has been welding three passages together. Again we observe that this is an act of narrative *composition*, not a mere pasting of differing narrative sections on top of each other (cf Rudin-O'Brasky). The materials with which he worked can still be recognised, but the result is not just the sum of the addition of those materials. In verse 22b we find one of the most famous *tiqqûnê sopᵉrîm* in the Hebrew Bible. Originally the text said that Yahweh, as opposed to the two departing companions, remained standing before Abraham. This gave offence to the later scribes because *'md lipnê* could, in later parlance, be taken to mean 'stand in the service of'. But the original text, suggesting as it does a daring picture of Abraham confronting God, would be fully in keeping with the bold theological stance assumed by Abraham and with the equally risky comment of Brueggemann who speaks of 'Abraham as Yahweh's theological instructor' (Brueggemann 1982:168).

Verses 23b-33. The conversation between Abraham and Yahweh is often seen as a supplication by Abraham on behalf of Sodom (cf Gunkel, Procksch, Von Rad, Zimmerli, Scharbert). But it is obviously not a supplication in the conventional sense where one party would beseech God to show mercy to another. The framework of the conversation is formed not by a plea and the granting of a request (cf Am 7:1-6, Jr 11:14), but by questions and answers (Westermann). On the other hand it is just as obvious that Abraham's conversation with Yahweh about justice, hingeing as it does on the fate of Sodom, makes him the *de facto* counsel for the defence as much as the spokesman for real divine justice. While Schmidt (1976:135) is right in rejecting the idea of intercessory prayer ('Fürbitte') as label for the passage, we can accept Vawter's description of Abraham as a mediator between God and man. Abraham takes the initiative and introduces the theme of the dialogue in his very first words (v 23b): *ha'ap tispè ṣaddîq 'im râšâ'*, 'Wilt thou sweep away the righteous with the wicked?' His own opinion is stated in a daring fivefold injunction (v 25):

A let it be far from thee to do such a thing
B to kill the righteous with the wicked
B so that the righteous becomes like the wicked
A let it be far from thee
› will the judge of all the earth not do justice?

The chiastic symmetry of these units, in which the first corresponds with the fourth and the second with the third, has the effect of an *inclusio* so that the last unit is isolated and emphasised. The rhetorical question in this unit affirms that it is expected of God to do justice. The theme is, therefore, the problem whether God discriminates between the righteous and the wicked when he metes out punishment, and Abraham's stance on the issue is that God is *supposed* to do so. Throughout the conversation Abraham remains respectful, but he consistently pushes his point without conceding an inch. So we have two forces juxtaposed in Abraham's contribution to the dialogue: deference as well as resoluteness. The implication that God is capable of injustice can be seen in the seriousness of Abraham's quest for justice. At stake is not only the fate of the Sodomites, but the concept of a just God. Abraham urges God not to make it impossible for him to believe in such a God by repeating the injunction *ḥâlilâ lⁱᵉkâ* (with *dâgèš forte firmativum*), made famous by Dillmann's Latin rendering: *profanum tibi sit*, 'let it be an unholy thing unto thee!' Abraham's case is enhanced by the *diminuendo* of the numbers employed in the argument and the conversely related *crescendo* of its force. By progressively reducing the number of righteous people required to save a doomed city, he first establishes the principle that the righteous should *not* be punished for the sins of the wicked and then reinforces the principle. Yahweh explicitly says several times that he will refrain from destroying the wicked city for the sake of (*baᵃᵇûr*) a righteous minority. This does not imply any atoning function of the minority, but only that the punishment will be abrogated (*nśʾ*; cf Stolz 1976:109-117) so that the righteous few can escape. It is often said that our passage is about the question whether the fate of communities is decided by the wicked mass or by the righteous few (e g Von Rad, who denies the presence of any element of protest against collectivism, and Van Seters 1975:214). Schmidt (1976:141) is correct when he stresses that the individual is in the focus of attention, but wrong when he takes Gunkel to task for not seeing this (Schmidt 1976:139-140). Gunkel (1910:204) explains at length that the problem is precipitated by the difficulty of the lot of the individual in cases where the destruction of whole communities is perceived as God's punishment. We should not counterpoise the 'collective' and the 'individual' perspectives, because the latter must necessarily be present where the problem is present (if one righteous individual perishes because of a wicked community, the problem arises), and the former must necessarily be present if it is deemed possible that the destruction may be abrogated on account of (*baᵃᵇûr*) the righteous. There is a third possibility, viz that only the righteous individuals themselves are saved whereas the wicked mass is justly punished. This is what happens in the Sodom story (Gn 19), and therefore it is quite understandable that Abraham's *diminuendo* stops at ten. Ten is the smallest number to make up a group (Schmidt 1976:154-155). The fact that Abraham stops here, does not mean that righteous individuals will have to perish if they number less than ten, but that they can be saved as individuals, which is evident in the rest of the story. If there were to be no punishment at all (which Brueggemann seems to be hinting at), then 'justice would be bereft of all meaning' (Vawter). Not even Job, who is the grand master of confrontation with God on the issue of justice, could question the idea of 'each receiving his or her due' (Brueggemann 1982:173).

Where is the quest for the preservation of God's righteousness to be placed in terms of the history of traditions? Westermann is quick to claim that it has its place in the complex of post-exilic proverbs about the fate of the righteous and the wicked. Now it is true that the ṣaddîq and the râšâʿ feature in many sayings of Proverbs 10-22. Even if we grant that these are late (cf H.H. Schmid 1966:155-169, who calls the tendency to categorise people an 'Anthropologisierung der Weisheit'), Westermann's main point remains that the fate of the wicked must be negative and that of the righteous must be positive. Not much is gained by this insight, for the principle of correlation of deed and consequence is much older than the exilic period. The whole religion of Israel only makes sense on this premise. As Crenshaw (1970:384) puts it: '... priest, prophet and wise man labored under the assumption of a correlation between good conduct and earthly reward.' So the recognition of the nexus between deed and consequence in the sapiential tradition of Israel in itself helps us very little. The fact that the nexus occurs right through Israel's religion and right through her history does show, however, that the foundations for the crisis were laid early in the history of Israel and not only in the post-exilic wisdom movement. This is another argument in favour of retaining the individualistic perspective on the problem (cf above). The sapiential application of the nexus of deed and consequence involves everyday ethics as the responsibility of the individual (cf Schmidt 1976:147-148; Gese 1962:1576).

It is quite possible that the crisis itself, the doubt about God's justice evident in Genesis 18:23-25, could have been precipitated by the fall of Samaria in 722 BCE. Everything that can be said in favour of the fall of Jerusalem in 587 BCE as the event that caused the problem of God's justice in relation to his acts in history, can also be said in favour of the fall of Samaria as such an event. Therefore it is not necessary to follow Westermann and Schmid in assigning a post-exilic date to the passage. It seems quite possible to think in terms of the eighth century.

For instance, Psalm 78 was obviously written after the fall of Samaria and refers both to that event and to Jerusalem which is still intact (cf Ps 78:67-69). It theologises about Yahweh's rejection of the Northern Kingdom from a Southern Kingdom perspective. There is, further, no reason to say that the crisis could not have been evoked in even earlier times by people observing discrepancies in the system (which did in fact happen at an early stage in Egypt and Mesopotamia; cf Scharbert). The same kind of awareness of God's deeds in history ('Geschichtshandeln') is also found in the Mesa Inscription from the ninth century BCE, where the deity is visualised as involving himself in the history of a city/nation (cf Albright 1955:320). In addition there is evidence of deuteronomic awareness of exactly the problem which interests us here, viz the lot of innocent people among a mass that is going to be killed. The fate of women, children and animals is handled with more sympathy that that of men (Dt 20:13-14). Behind this law lie very old traditions of the so-called Yahweh wars. This makes it possible that we have before us proto-deuteronomic ideas from the Northern Kingdom of about the eighth century BCE. By this I do not mean that the Sodom story itself is deuteronomic, which would have required the presence of a prophet to warn the wicked beforehand, but that the agonising over Yahweh's justice to the innocent in the event of mass destruction may be related to deuteronomic thought. At least it shows that the problem was thought about and theologised about before the exile.

So Schmidt and Westermann are not right in claiming that the problem of Yahweh's justice in its connexion with his acts in history only comes to the fore since the fall of Jerusalem in 587 BCE. This event certainly had all the ingredients to cause the enigma of how God's justice can be squared with the belief that he controlled the fate of nations, but so did the fall of Samaria and even the fate of communities in earlier Israelite history. If Yahweh could bring the Assyrians to Samaria, if Chemosh could bring the Moabites against Nebo (cf Albright 1955:320), and if the deuteronomic law of wars could reflect on the lot of minority groups in cities, then the whole concept of Yahweh's 'Geschichtshandeln' and its relationship to the problem of our passage is thoroughly thinkable in the pre-exilic period.

Moreover, the classic prophets of the eighth and seventh centuries obviously work with the presupposition that Yahweh controls the history of nations and that he does so according to the principle of deed and consequence. But the other side of the coin is that he is also supposed to control the lot of individuals whose deeds do not warrant death or captivity. How is this to be explained? Why did these good people also undergo the effects of God's wrath?

The question is answered in various texts from this period. In Ezekiel 18 we find a classic exposition of the correlation of deed and consequence with reference to the idea of individual responsibility. Collective guilt and collective merit are explicitly rejected. The same is found in Ezekiel

14:12-20. Here it is said that not even the classic types of meritoriousness, Noah, Daniel and Job, would be able to save a community of wicked people, but that they would only save themselves. Usually this protest against collectivism is regarded as an escape from the consequences of a 'primitive' corporate view of human destiny. But it is an escape directly into the problem of justice and therefore of theodicy: What if individuals are innocent and in fact are not saved? From a collective perspective the problem does not arise, but from an individualist perspective it grows into a conflict in which nothing less than the concept of God and a moral world order is at stake. Different answers are possible.

It could be maintained bluntly that the nexus of deed and consequence works in spite of all appearances. This is the option of Job's friends whose exposition is developed in the dialogues of Job 3-27.

The nexus could also be doubted before being affirmed in the end. This is not such a doctrinaire position as that of Job's friends, but ultimately it is accepted that somehow good deeds will be rewarded and bad deeds will be punished. This is found in the agony of poems like Psalms 37, 49 and 73. Schmid (1966:235-239) adds several examples from Mesopotamia.

A third possibility would be to categorically deny the existence of all retributive justice. This can be done while maintaining an explicit faith in the unfathomable depths of God's moral order, which is what happens in the Book of Job (cf Job 38-42). It can also be done with profound pessimism in spite of the element of wonder, which is what Qohelet does (cf Ecc 8:14, 9:1-3.11 in spite of 3:11).

A fourth type of reaction to the problem would be what we have in Genesis 18:17-33. Here we find the problem itself on two levels and therefore an answer on two levels. The one could be called the collective level. It is repeatedly stated that a community can be saved on account of (ba"bûr) a small group of righteous people. A little goodness outweighs much wickedness. This is the exact opposite of the emphatic denial of Ezekiel (cf Ezk 14:14), and conversely related to Qohelet's pessimistic notion that a little of the negative force in life outweighs much of the positive force (Ecc 10:1-2). The other level in our passage could be called the individual level. Abraham is made to discontinue his *diminuendo* of numbers at ten to show that no righteous group is to be found in Sodom. But the story goes on to show that the good Lot himself is saved. His wife perishes on their way out, which is her own fault and not that of the wicked community (cf below, p 41). All of this goes to show that our author – for that is what the creator of the conversation between Abraham and Yahweh is – believed that individual retribution does occur. He establishes that 'the power of righteousness overrides evil' (Brueggemann 1982:172), but also the principle of 'each receiving his or her due' (denied by Brueggemann 1982:173). Not even Job himself questions this principle. On the contrary, his whole argument against God is based on exactly this premise. Neither does our author have a bone to pick with Ezekiel (or Jr 31:29-30) on this principle. He only contests the notion that it is applied so blindly that minorities are overlooked.

For the reasons given above I cannot concur with Westermann (and many others) in assigning an exilic date to the passage (cf also Schmid 1976:151-152). His argument based on Proverbs, Job and God's activity in history is not nuanced enough and lacks depth. This also goes for the rather blunt way in which many commentators declare our passage to be a reflexion on a theoretical problem and the work of some 'group of redactors' (cf Dentan 1963:34-51). The narrator who is responsible for this passage used the older stories of the visit to Abraham by three men and of the destruction of Sodom skilfully. We have seen this in the way he engineered the flowing over of the one into the other. It is also evident in the way in which the abrupt ending of the episode at a group of ten is supplemented by the rescue of individuals in the next chapter. Therefore the author of this passage must be the one who welded the whole Sodom Cycle together. This is further borne out by the fact that our passage does not only link well with the sections preceding and following it, but also with its counterpart in Genesis 19:27-29, (cf above, pp 16: 'Prelude' [B] and 'Aftermath' [B']). The preliminary conclusion reached at the end of paragraph 2.1 (p 26) is therefore augmented by what we have found here: Old, pre-Israelite material was reworked into a Yahwistic story and, in late pre-exilic times, moulded with original 'reflective' material to form the Sodom Cycle. This conclusion undermines the usual view that the Sodom story proper is to be ascribed to the so-called Yahwist of early monarchic times, while Genesis 18:17-33 is ascribed to an exilic author who is supposed to have undergone Deuteronomistic influence (cf above, p 31).

2.3. God's wrath over Sodom (Gn 19:1-26)

The story of the destruction of Sodom and Gomorrah can be divided into three episodes, viz Genesis 19:1-11, 12-22, 23-26. It ends at verse 26 because Abraham, who is absent troughout the three sections, is reintroduced in verse 27. In this way the Sodom events are encircled by Abraham's preview and his review of the disaster. The structure initially resembles that of Genesis 18:1-16:

I Two men visit Lot (vv 1-11)
   A. Introductory statement (v 1a)
   B. Arrival of the visitors (v 1b-c)
   C. Lot's hospitality
      i) Invitation (v 2)
      ii) Reception (v 3)
   D. Confrontation after the meal
      i) Lot and the mob (vv 4-9)
      ii) The messengers and the mob (vv 10-11)

II Lot saved (vv 12-22)
   A. The men speak (vv 12-13)
   B. Lot acts (v 14)
   C. The men speak (v 15)
   D. The men act (v 16)
   E. Dialogue between God and Lot (vv 17-22)

III Collective and individual destruction (vv 23-26)
   A. Time (v 23)
   B. The cities destroyed (vv 24-25)
   C. Lot's wife destroyed (v 26)

The structure of verses 1-3 and that of Genesis 18:1-8 have many similarities. Both Kilian (1966:150-151) and Van Seters (1975:215-216) have drawn up tables showing the far-reaching parallels which even extend to the very words used. Both passages begin with an introductory statement about the appearance of Yahweh/angels, both continue with their arrival, being seen, greeted and invited, and both describe the hospitality extended to them. A difference is that the men in Genesis 18 stand as if waiting for an invitation (Delitzsch), whereas the men here at first decline the invitation and only accept after being urged to do so. The latter trait is, again, identical to what is found in the third parallel passage in the Old Testament, Judges 19:15-25, which is closely similar to Genesis 19. In our passage a serious confrontation follows the meal, while a far less serious one follows the meal in Genesis 18. The motifs of acting and speaking are symmetrically organised in verses 4-9:

A mob acts (v 4)
B mob speaks (v 5)

Lot acts (v 6)
Lot speaks (vv 7-8)

B mob speaks (v 9a-b)
A mob acts (v 9c-d)

The *inclusio* isolates the action of the men which follows in verses 10-11. The structure of the second main part of the passage, verses 12-22, mirrors the element of suspense in the contents: The messengers speak (vv 12-13), Lot speaks (v 14), then the messengers speak again (v 15), then they act (v 16), then Lot involves himself in a lengthy dialogue with Yahweh (vv 17-21). This verbosity prolongs the tension like in a nightmare where the urgently needed movement never seems to materialise. Sharply opposed to this lengthy run-up, the destruction itself is described in a few short sentences (Part III).

Verse 1. The two messengers who arrive in Sodom are the two men who have left Abraham and Yahweh (Gn 18:22, cf 18:16). Here they are called 'messengers', 'angels' (*mal'ākîm*). This feature of the passage is often called a later explanation which replaced an earlier reference to two or three 'men' (*ᵃnāšîm*) (cf, among others, Dillmann, Gunkel, Skinner, Westermann). Van Seters (1975:216) has correctly seen that this is a sensible act of the narrator, but his idea that it demonstrates 'the complete fantasy' of a process of oral tradition is not borne out by the evidence. The activity of a literary narrator responsible for this kind of 'change' (?) in the text does not exclude the possibility of oral traditions preceding such work. The fact that it would have taken the men some two days (instead of one afternoon, cf *bâ'èrèb*) to complete the journey from Mamre to Sodom need not in itself prove, as Westermann thinks, that the two stories were originally separate. From a narrative point of view the distance is unimportant and therefore no thought is given to the time it would normally take. Lot does what Abraham had done by going towards the men, prostrating himself before them (cf Gn 18:2). There is nothing different, as Speiser contends, in his bowing 'with his face to the ground'; how could he have held his face otherwise?

Verses 2-3. Lot's hospitality is also very similar to his uncle's. He begs the messengers to be his guests. The difference here is that the men decline, whereas in Abraham's case they stood waiting for an invitation (cf Gn 18:2 – *niṣṣâbîm*). It is rather unfair to Lot when Speiser calls him 'servile...as contrasted with the simple dignity of Abraham'. Lot is pictured as a man who respects the sacred duty of hospitality. If anything, he even surpasses Abraham because of his insistence and because of the fact that he himself does the baking while Abraham orders his wife to do so. The words informing us about his willingness to do even women's work (cf Gunkel on Gn 18:6!) are organised chiastically and therefore draw attention (verb - object - object - verb).

36

Verses 4-9. The next section bears out that Lot is a meritorious man. When the mob of Sodom arrives at his door, it is specifically stressed that not one of the men of the city was absent:

the men of the city
the men of Sodom
from the youngest to the oldest
the whole population (*kol hâ'âm*)
until the last man (*miqqâ sè*)

The fivefold statement makes it difficult to follow the many commentators who hold that *'anšê s^edom* is a gloss. On the contrary, the heavy emphasis on the presence of *all* the men is an important indicator of the fact that the whole city is guilty and that they do not deserve to be saved. Their sin is a three-in-one matter. They violate the sacred law of *hospitality* and in so doing give themselves over to *depravity of a homosexual nature* (cf Lv 18:22, 20:13). At the same time it must be said that the sin here is not just a private homosexual act, but homosexual *mob rape* (cf Brueggemann 1982:164). The fact that Lot is prepared to surrender his virgin daughters rather than his guests to the lust of the mob suggests that the emphasis is on the social aspect of their sin and not on the sexual aspect itself. This is how Josephus and the rabbis interpreted the wickedness of Sodom (cf below, pp 101, 112). Instead of moralising about this shocking aspect of Lot's fatherhood (as older commentators were sometimes prone to do) or arguing against such moralising (of which later commentators are sometimes fond), we should recognise the literary function of this motif. It highlights the fact that sexual misdemeanour, even though it certainly is part of the sin of 'sodomy', is not the central or most important part. The Sodomites are engaging in an anti-social act of violence and oppression. It is not for nothing that this is expressed in the motif of *perverse* sex. This is not only to show that the Sodomites wanted to 'humiliate and "demasculinize" the guests' (as Shafer 1984:773 calls it). The Sodomites make natural intercourse impossible by violating the social fibre of the community as represented by the motif of hospitality. They *pervert* the natural obligations by which life in ancient communities was made possible. It is therefore expressed by means of an appropriate narrative vehicle, viz the motif of sex in which the natural intercourse is likewise *perverted* and expressly *denied* (when Lot's offer of his daughters is turned down). Lot's going out and speaking in defence of his guests is an act of courage (vv 6-8). In this way an important contrast is created: The merit of the individual is counterpoised to the sin of the collective community. This is confirmed by the reaction of the mob (v 9): They unrepentingly stick to their intentions in spite of the accommodating way in which Lot approaches them (cf *'aḥay* in v 7 and the offer of his daughters in v 8) and they threaten Lot with worse treatment than his visitors (*nāra' l'kâ mehèm*). This proves that the over-arching element of their vice is violence. The double *wayyô'm'rû* in verse 9 is not at all a clumsy vestige of earlier 'sources'; it serves as a kind of distributive formula to suggest the distribution of the different cries coming from different sections of the crowd, one group using the second person and one the third person.

Three further aspects of this section are important for their bearing on the compositional context.

First, the mentioning of Lot's daughters at this point prepare the way for the last passage in the Sodom Cycle (Gn 19:30-38; cf Gunkel). In that passage they play the major role over against their pathetic father, whose relationship to them is already flawed here in spite of his courage.

Second, the wickedness of the Sodomites is described quite clearly so as to confirm the rumours about them. In the previous passage we were told that Yahweh had heard claims about the wickedness of Sodom and Gomorrah, and that he wanted to find out whether these were true (Gn 18:22). Here nothing is said about Gomorrah, but we are left in no doubt as to the truth of those rumours in Sodom's case.

Third, the sinfulness of life in the city is contrasted with the rustic virtue of hospitality found in nomadic society (cf Wallis 1966:144-145) and depicted in the opening passage of the Sodom Cycle (Abraham as a nomad in Gn 18:1-16). Abraham and his environment stand over against the men of Sodom and their environment, while Lot, showing as he does respect for the nomadic ideals, is presented as a tragic illustration that the nomad way of life is not tolerated in the city. The defence of nomad or at least rural morals is looked upon as arrogance ('this outsider wants to act as judge', v 9). We may therefore speak of an anti-urban tendency in the story.

Verses 10-11. The supernatural powers of the guests become apparent at the crucial point. When Lot's measures prove ineffectual they step in. The men who are supposed to be under Lot's protection take him under theirs. Lot who took them into his house (*bw'* Qal, v 3) is now taken into his own house by them (*bw'* Hif'il, v 10). Then they blind the mob so that these cannot find the door. This motif is found elsewhere in the Ancient Near East (cf Gaster 1969:158-159, who cites, among others, examples from Dt 28:28, 2 Ki 6:18, the Ugaritic Aqhat Text, and Babylonian and Old South Arabian curses). The blindness is something unusual, since an uncommon word is used for it – not the root *'wr*, but *sanwerîm*, possibly an Akkadian loanword (cf Speiser). Once again it is stressed that every single man of Sodom was involved and so they all deserved what happened to them.

Verses 12-14. The second main episode of the Sodom passage proper begins at verse 12. We will discuss the first two sections (respectively vv 12-13 and v 14) together. The messengers (*mal'âkîm*) of verse 1 are called 'men' (*ˀanâšîm*), as they are in verse 10 as well. Their injunction that Lot should get any other relatives he may have (v 12) out of the city, prepares the introduction of his sons-in-law-to-be (v 14), which again serves the purpose of the last passage of the cycle where the daughters have no husbands (Gn 19:30-38). Of course they scoff, because according to verses 4 and 11 they too must have been among the mob. Again we hear about the clamour (this time written with *ṣâdè*, cf the *zâyin* in Gn 18:20). The plural suffix can only refer to the inhabitants of the city and can be taken as a *constructio ad sensum*, which means that Westermann is wrong in stating that it cannot suit *hammâqôm hazzè*. In these verses too we encounter the plural and the singular for God's action, which Kilian (1966, cf above on Gn 18:1-16) ascribes to different sources. However, here we can counter his thesis in the same way as earlier. In verse 13 the men say that they themselves are on the verge of destroying the city, and in verse 14 Lot says that Yahweh is going to do so. The narrator thus shows that Lot understood the reference of the men to their task as a reference to what Yahweh is going to do. This is explained at the end of verse 13 by the words that Yahweh has sent the men. The deity's own interest in the matter and that of his messengers are merged, which should not surprise us after what we have found in Genesis 18:1-16.

Verses 15-16. Beginning with the solemn *kᵉmô* – a sign that things are becoming very serious – we are told that daybreak has in the meantime arrived. Time is running out fast (cf v 23, where it is said that the destruction itself took place at sunrise, i e soon afterwards). Suspense is heightened by the fact that the messengers (v 15) or men (v 16) have to urge Lot and that he still hesitates. This goes on until number ninety-nine, when the men are compelled to save Lot and his family by physically removing them from their house, in contrast to the way that they earlier had to save Lot by physically bringing him *into* his own house (v 10). They actually have to take trouble to save Lot, which is highlighted by the words *ḥemlat yhwh*. Not only these words refer back to Genesis 18:24-32 (so Procksch, following Dillmann), but the whole theme of the conversation between Abraham and Yahweh is concentrated here in the words *pen tissâpè baˁᵃwon hâˁîr*, 'so that you are not swept away because of the wickedness/guilt of the city' (well translated by Gunkel). It is not important to the argument which meaning of *ˁâwon* is the one intended, but it is important to notice that *tissâpè* is singular and *hâˁîr* is collective. Yahweh's purpose is that the innocent individual should not be punished because of the guilt of the mass. That was the thrust of the previous passage, which is now shown to be applied practically in Sodom.

Verses 17-22. Another dialogue follows. Lot and his family are now left to themselves, but they have a divine injunction to guide them. *wayyô'mèr* is singular and obviously refers to Yahweh. The oscillation of singular and plural which we have been studying now enters its final phase. Lot is to flee and is neither allowed to look back nor to stop until he has reached the mountains. The imperatives are chiastically organised: positive – negative – negative – positive and therefore catch the eye. The second person masculine singular addressed to Lot also applies to his family, as the injunction not to look back and the event mentioned in verse 26 show. Again the suspense is heightened by the lengthy speech by Lot. He addresses the men (v 18: *ᵃlêhèm*, plural), but, as he continues, we find him addressing someone in the second person *singular* (v 19: *'abdᵉkâ, bᵉ'ènèkâ, wattagdel, ḥasdᵉkâ, 'âśîtâ*). The plural in verse 18 need not be explained as a 'harmonisation' (Westermann), but is the final touch of the author's technique of keeping the figure of Yahweh nebulous throughout the narrative. Yahweh is addressed as if he were present all along (Fripp 1892:24). In line with his explanation of this phenomenon in Genesis 18:1-16, Procksch comments: 'Also vollzieht J während des Gesprächs unmerklich einen Uebergang zum Singular...'. He is probably also right when he sees in the suffix with *qâmèṣ*, which refers to God, an easy development from the suffix with *pataḥ*, which would indicate more than one man being addressed (*ᵃdonây* instead of *ᵃdonay*). Lot asks another favour from Yahweh, viz to be allowed to flee to the nearby town of Zoar rather than to have to go to the mountains beyond. He repeatedly mentions the town's smallness as substantiation for his request. In addition to the impact of depicting the pathetic entreaty of a man who will reach for any argument, the explanation of the name of the town *ṣo'ar* by *miṣ'âr* ('small') is prepared (cf v 22). Yahweh grants his request by saying that he has favoured Lot 'also in this matter' and that he will not destroy Zoar. *gam* does not, as Westermann thinks, imply that the first favour was preceded by a request also; it refers to the favour of being saved from Sodom. In this way Yahweh's extraordinary grace is underlined. This must be an old and established element in the tradition, because it implies that the people of Zoar were to have been destroyed but are now to be saved on account of Lot, an individual. The matter should not be pressed, however, because the wickedness of the people of Zoar is not an issue like that of the inhabitants of Sodom and Gomorrah. Rather, the etiological purpose is served of explaining both the name (cf the last sentence in v 22) and the continued existence of the town on the southeastern side of the Dead Sea (cf Gn 13:10, 14:2.8, Dt 34:3, Is 15:5, Jr 48:34).

Verses 23-26. By mentioning the time of the destruction, which equals the time of Lot's arrival in Zoar (cf v 22), the narrator lets us see retrospectively how narrowly Lot managed to escape. The motif of speed need not be explained by assuming that the destruction at sunrise was brought about by the sun god (Keel 1979:10-17). It is sufficiently accounted for as a narrative technique which produces tension. Here Gomorrah is mentioned together with Sodom, whereas the author has focussed on Sodom right through his story. Not the men, as said in verse 13, but Yahweh himself brings about the destruction (cf Gunkel). The 'rain' of sulphur and fire on the cities (v 24) and the verb 'overturn' (hpk) are not at all difficult to reconcile as claimed by Dillmann and Westermann. The verb points to an earthquake (Procksch, Speiser) and the sulphurous rain to volcanic activity (Gunkel), which are quite compatible (cf, further, below).

The reference to Lot's wife in verse 26 may i a have been an etiological element which explained some bizarre figure in the rock formations near the Dead Sea (cf Dillmann, Gunkel, Von Rad; Harland 1942:23-26 discusses at some length the salt-mass Jebel Usdum and its association with our story). The injunction not to look back is, however, more than that. It is a widespread motif found often in the folklore of widely differing cultures (cf Rudin-O'Brasky, Gaster 1969:159-160). In our story it serves an important purpose. Lot's wife meets her end because of her own, individual transgression of the express command given in verse 17. In other words, it confirms the theme of the dialogue between God and Abraham and in the mainline narrative of Genesis 19: If human beings are punished by Yahweh, it is because of their own fault, not because of that of a community (cf above, pp 33-34).

In this central part of the Sodom Cycle we find evidence of very ancient traditional material and of the period from which the narrative as a composition hails.

The first part of the passage (vv 1-11) is closely parallelled by Judges 19:15-25, a historical narrative from the time of the early settlement of Israel in Canaan. The differences and even the contrast between the two should also be respected: In Genesis the emphasis falls on Lot's being saved from the destruction, in Judges on the expedition against Gibea; in Genesis it is God who causes a natural catastrophe, in Judges humans do the punishing (Westermann; cf Lasine 1984:37-59). The Sodom Cycle comes from a time later than the Judges passage, when old material was incorporated in a well planned narrative.

The rain of fire and sulphur (v 24) strongly suggests volcanic activity. The fact that the latest volcanic activity in the south of the Dead Sea area took place long before the second millennium BCE (cf Clapp 1936:323-344), is only a problem for a reader who wishes to associate a historical patriarch with a historical event (cf Harland 1943:43; for the question of the site in general, cf Lagrange 1932:489-514; Van Hattem 1981:87-92 thinks the Pentapolis can be identified with cites south of the Dead Sea if we date the 'events' – including the association of the patriarchs with the cities – back well into the third millennium). We should rather see in our story evidence of the reminiscence of an ancient experience which made an indelible impact on the collective memory of the inhabitants of the region where it took place (cf Kilian 1966:135, Zimmerli, Westermann). The whole plain is affected by the catastrophe (v 25). This fact, as well as the reference to Gomorrah, which is mentioned often in the biblical tradition of the destruction but which is not at all prominent in our narrative, shows that we here have the oldest part of the narrative. It has been used as the central motif of the traditions brought together in the Sodom Cycle. Since time immemorial it has made its way into various traditions and thus also into the seventh century story that we have before us. It is the theological expression of an ancient experience. Kilian (1966:133-134) adds that for this reason it is wrong to relocate the tradition to a place where volcanic activity could indeed have been possible, as Gunkel does. I agree that verses 24-25 show a theologising tendency, but we do not need this insight as an argument to explain the 'rain of fire and sulphur' – it is merely an element of the reminiscence of an ancient event which Kilian (1966:135) himself regards as quite possibly having occurred. Whether the experience which gave rise to the tradition took place in the Dead Sea region before historical times or whether it was transferred there from another place, cannot be decided. We only have a tradition which explains the region's inhospitable character and which, for that reason, must be very old.

In Genesis 13 we find an Israelite tradition of the relationship between Abraham and Lot as well as the settling of Lot in Sodom. The Sodom Cycle as we have it presupposes this. Therefore our author also must have had to make use of these Israelite traditions to build up his story. He was not the one who associated the tradition of the destruction of the Dead Sea plain with Israel's patriarchs, but he was the one who reworked this early Israelite tradition into the shape and with the meaning it has in Genesis 18-19. The balanced structure and coherent meaning of the story make it inadvisable to claim with Van Seters (1975:221-222) that Genesis 13 and 18-19 were once a *literary* unit (cf Gunkel 1910:175 on Gn 13:10). There were narratives in circulation about Abraham, Lot and Sodom, but also about Gomorrah and the whole Jordan valley (Gn 13:10-12). These may have been in oral or in written form. Be that as it may, the author of the Sodom Cycle was not merely an editor who severed the introduction of the story (Gn 13, which itself shows signs of different traditional perspectives – cf below, pp 51-53) from the rest (Gn 18-19). He was an *author* who could discard the original

42

beginning of the tradition (something like Gn 13) in order to rework a polytheistic story, compose a dialogue about God's justice and weld all of this together with the old traditional material into his own story around the theme of punishment and justice (Gn 18-19).

We have seen that our passage bears evidence of an anti-urban attitude (cf p 38). This points to a pre-exilic time for the cycle as a whole. The latest evidence that could be interpreted as anti-urban is found in Jeremiah's example of the Rechabites (Jr 35). Since the composer of the complete cycle is the one who created the careful contrast between the rustic Abraham and the urban Sodomites, as well as the figure of Lot as the tragic link between the two, he will have to be dated in the pre-exilic period. If we allow sufficient time during the monarchy for the development of this kind of social conflict and the resulting moral conflict, the most likely period would be the eighth/seventh century (cf above, pp 31-34). This conclusion supports the direction taken by Schmid (1976) in his objections to the early dating of J, whose work, according to a wide consensus of opinion, is also found in the Sodom story. My analysis, if accepted, would add another argument to those developed throughout his book (cf the concluding examples, 1976:154-166), although I would not prefer a date for the Sodom Cycle quite as late as the early sixth century BCE even if this still qualifies as pre-exilic (cf p 65 on Ezekiel's dependence on the Sodom Cycle).

Our narrative depicts an anti-social deed of oppression against helpless wanderers (we may even call them *gerîm*). Therefore there is no fundamental difference between the view taken here of Sodom's sin and that of the prophets who emphasise its social aspect (cf i.a. Is 1:10-17, Jr 23:14, Ezek 16:48-49; below, pp 59 ff).

2.4. Abraham witnesses the destruction (Gn 19:27-29)

These verses form the counterpart of Genesis 18:17-33. I have argued (pp 15-16) that the author of the Sodom Cycle has thus created an inner circle around the destruction story proper, and that in so doing he has integrated the Sodom story into the Abraham story (Skinner and Procksch call this 'an impressive close'). Westermann is to be agreed with when he remarks that these verses have a different character from Genesis 18:17-33. There will of course be such a difference when the one is a dialogue and the other a short description. Structurally they have in common, however, that both involve Abraham and that the first is a prelude to the destruction while the other looks back at the aftermath of the catastrophe. The passage consists of a reference to Abraham's looking (vv 27-28a), to what he actually saw (v 28b), and a short summary of the story (v 29). The latter verse is often regarded as a priestly addition. It may well be such, since it adds nothing essential to the story, since it substantiates Lot's escape differently, and since the incorporation of the Sodom tradition into the Abraham tradition is sufficiently performed by verses 27-28.

Verses 27-28 suggest an uneasiness in Abraham. This makes the link with his earlier dialogue quite effective (cf Procksch: Abraham was already uneasy in his discussion with God). Since speaking to Yahweh he has therefore been apprehensive of what was going to happen. In spite of the fact that Yahweh had earlier decided not to hide his plan from Abraham (Gn 18:17), even Abraham did not know exactly what the result of his discussion with Yahweh would be. Here again Gomorrah is mentioned together with Sodom and the whole plain, which is a clear indication of its being part of an earlier tradition used by the author.

Verse 29 goes further than anything that we find in the Sodom Cycle in giving an interpretation of the story: The saving of Lot took place for the sake of Abraham. God (*'elohîm*) 'thought of Abraham' and therefore saved the latter's nephew from the catastrophe. This differs markedly from the grappling with the problem of God's justice found in Genesis 18:17-33. Lot was not saved because of Yahweh's justice, but because of his kinship to God's chosen one. While verses 27-28 relate to Genesis 18:17-33, verse 29 relates to something outside the Sodom Cycle, viz Abraham's chosenness and his relationship to Lot (cf Gn 12:1-5).

The repetitive character of verse 29 shows that it is an addition. Its interest in Abraham suggests a priestly perspective on our seventh-century narrative and therefore it must be dated later, probably in exilic times. According to Speiser, who also regards Gn 18-19, with the exception of this verse, as the product of one author, the priestly style of verse 29 'is an example of scholastic succinctness at its best'.

2.5. Lot and his daughters (Gn 19:30-38)

The concluding passage of the Sodom Cycle harks back to the opening passage in that the antecedent is about Abraham's offspring and the postscript about the offspring of his relatives (cf above, p 16). In both cases the continued existence of the family is in jeopardy, but in the case of Abraham the matter is resolved by divine intervention while Lot's daughters take matters into their own hands.

The passage is built up as follows:

A. Introduction: itinerary (v 30)
B. The daughters and their father
   i) The elder's intention and deed (vv 31-33)
   ii) The younger's intention and deed (vv 34-35)

C. Consequence
   i) Pregnancies (v 36)
   ii) The elder (v 37)
   iii) The younger (v 38)

The rigid structure is a reflection of the fact that there are two daughters and that the one's fate is parallel to the other's; whatever happens to the one happens to the other as well.

Verse 30. Westermann points out that the itinerary, in its connexion with the Sodom narrative, is parallelled by the itinerary of Lot found in Genesis 13:11-12, which also is associated with Sodom and its wickedness (Gn 13:13). Even Zoar seems unsafe to Lot; he has enough reason to mistrust city life (cf above, p 37-38) and he moves into the mountains farther east, that is, farther from Canaan (cf below p 49). According to the Masoretic text he goes to a specific cave known to the narrator and to his readers (*bamm^e'ârâ* has the definite article).

Verses 31-33. It is said that there is no man left on earth, which suggests a complete catastrophe (Gunkel, Skinner; Lods 1927:204-219). In view of the context in which the destruction is limited to the cities of the plain (v 29) this cannot, however, be the opinion of the narrator (cf Procksch). We therefore probably have an old tradition incorporated by our author in the Sodom story to serve as his concluding section. Rather than indulge in moral verdicts over the incest of the daughters (which is done by Dillmann; cf Von Rad), we should recognise that the survival of the human race or at least, in the present context, of the family is at stake. Whether this 'adds up to praise rather than blame' (Speiser) is debatable, but it explains with sympathy (Rudin-O'Brasky) the desperate measure of the girls. The drunkenness of Lot would in any case extenuate his position and the passage should therefore not be taken as derogatory to Moab and Ammon who would then be 'incestuous' nations (cf Kilian 1966:138).

Verses 34-35. The same events happen all over again, and once more Lot knows nothing about it. His pathetic figure relates to his performance in Genesis 19:8 (cf above p 37). There is some bitter irony in this scene: The girls are obliged to have sex with their father who previously felt obliged to sacrifice them to the sexual lust of the Sodomites (cf Van Seters 1975:219). First too many men, and now none at all.

Verses 36-38. The sons born to the girls are the ancestors of the Moabites and the Ammonites. The etymological explanations of the names of these nations are ingeniously connected to the story: *mô'âb/me'âb* ('from father') and *b^{e}nê 'ammôn/bèn 'ammî* ('son of my relative'). In this way the story provides an explanation of the origins of Israel's neighbours (cf Van Seters 1975:220). The descendants of Abraham's relatives (spoken of in this passage) are now the neighbours of his own descendants (through the son spoken of in the first passage of the cycle).

According to Westermann the explanation of the origins of Moab and Ammon are only possible after the birth of these nations and can therefore not antedate Israel. However, Lods (1927:214) and Noth (1948:169) regard it likely on geographical grounds that Lot was seen as the ancestor of a pre-Moabite group and that this was only taken over by the Moabites at a later stage of the tradition. According to Kilian (1970:31) this was augmented still later by the addition of the Ammonites. On the other hand the motif of survival after a catastrophe is very old and may reflect a Moabite parallel to the deluge stories of the Ancient Near East (cf Skinner). So, apart from the latter possibility, the traditional material with which our author operates here dates at least from the pre-monarchical period. It has to be placed in the time when the Israelite tribes stood confronted with their Moabite and Ammonite neighbours, and that would make a time around the twelfth century sensible.

We can no longer reconstruct these traditions, but it cannot be denied that there are indications of their presence. Therefore I shall end the discussion of the biblical Sodom story by referring to what I said earlier (cf p 24) about Van Seters' view. Even if we cannot reconstruct the detail of a tradition (cf Van Seters 1975:157), we can explain much of a text like the Sodom Cycle by using the hypothesis of traditions. And at the same time we can appreciate the 'highly literate' skill of the author (cf Van Seters 1975:210) who moulded together such traditional materials in an artistic unit such as the Sodom Cycle.

2.6. Conclusions

We may now briefly summarise the results to which the analysis and argument of this chapter have led:

Genesis 18-19 is a skilfully composed narrative, moulded by an author from the monarchical period, probably during the seventh century BCE. This tends to support Schmid's argument in favour of a later date for the so-called Yahwist. Although the early sixth century is probably too late for the Sodom Cycle, it does suit its incorporation into what may be called the redactional J-tradition (cf Schmid 1976 and the argument below on the literary dependence of Ezekiel on the cycle, p 65).

The Sodom Cycle, as I have called it, is *organised* as a narrative text. The *function* of this text is to argue that God punishes wickedness, but that he also respects individual innocence in the midst of mass guilt, so that it is even possible that the guilty may be saved because of the innocent. Mass as well as individual guilt is punished, but not at the price of justice. So God is vindicated in the face of doubt about his righteousness when he intervenes in the affairs of humans.

Our author has made use of material from old traditions. I would agree with Rudin-O'Brasky that the author (called 'J' by her in accordance with classical historical criticism) was not just a compiler. So much must be clear from my analysis and argument in this chapter. However, the traditional material used by him should not be seen in terms of literary units like 'chapter 18' and 'chapter 19' which our author combined by using pasting-materials like Genesis 18:16.17-19.22.23-32.33 (which is what the view of Rudin-O'Brasky amounts to). In this way his composition is still regarded as the work of a compiler, albeit a skilful one. I have argued against this approach, in principle that of Van Seters, all along. The narrator was an *author* who created a story not by editing texts, but by making use of traditional lore or a variety of traditions known to him. The oldest among these are the traditions of the destruction of the cities of the Dead Sea plain underlying the story of the devastation proper in Genesis 19:23-26 and 27-28 (where the mentioning of Gomorrah and the plain betrays a wider interest than Sodom alone, on which our author focusses). These reminiscences, whether 'transferred' from other localities or not, come from times immemorial.

In our narrative we find both Israelite and non-Israelite material from the pre-monarchical period. In Genesis 18:1-16 we have evidence of a polytheistic story from pre-Israelite times which was handled by our author in such a way that it keeps the reader in uncertainty about Yahweh's presence. In Genesis 19:30-38 we also have pre-monarchical traditions about the origins of Moab and Ammon. They were probably taken over by Israel from these tribes themselves. The Israelite tradition of Abraham, his kinsman, and the settling of Lot in Sodom (underlying Gn 13 and 18-19) also comes from the tribal period. This means that the association of the patriarchs and the evil city was already known in Israel before the composition of the narrative as we know it. The author moulded all of this into a well-structured whole with a freedom which is most clearly seen in Genesis 18:17-33, where he introduces his own perspective in a way which is seminal for understanding the meaning of the composition as a whole.

Except for one of the famous *tiqqûnê sop^{e}rîm* in Genesis 18:22, the only real later addition to the story is the repetitive verse in Genesis 19:29, which reflects an exilic priestly interest in the merit of Abraham.

So we can recognise at least five layers of tradition in our text:
1. Ancient reminiscences of a catastrophe in the Dead Sea plain.

2. Different non-Israelite traditions from the pre-monarchical period (the visit by three gods; the origin of Israel's eastern neighbours).

3. An Israelite tradition of Abraham and the settlement of his kinsman in Sodom (which had already contained the idea of wickedness and punishment).

4. The author's own perspective from the seventh century BCE on punishment and God's justice.

5. One priestly addition from exilic times.

In terms of this summary, the redactional incorporation of the story into 'J' should be placed between 4. and 5.

This situation may be sketched as follows:

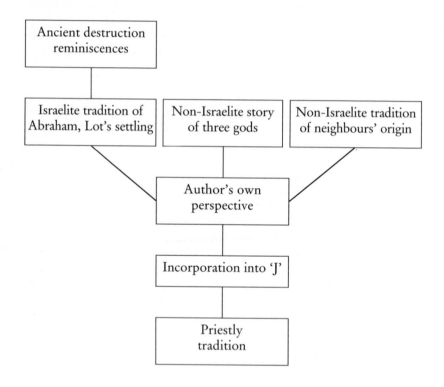

3. Sodom and Gomorrah in the rest of the Old Testament

We now turn to the other passages in the Old Testament where mention is made of Sodom and Gomorrah. We shall find that other cities are associated with them to form one tradition complex.

3.1. The Book of Genesis

Apart from the Sodom narrative in Genesis 18-19 mention is made of Sodom and Gomorrah in Genesis 10:19, 13:10.12.13, 14:2.8.10.11.12. 17.21.22.

Genesis 10:19 is part of the so-called Table of Peoples. As it stands, the reference to the cities occurs in the description of a geographical line from the northwest of Canaan to the southwest and thence to the southeast: 'And the boundary of the Caananites ran from Sidon as one goes to Gerar as far as Gaza, as one goes to Sodom and Gomorrah and Admah and Zeboim as far as Lasha.' There are some problems in this description. The location of Lasha is not known; it is, however, not necessary to emend the text to read *lešâ* = *layiš* + *he locale* in order to complete the boundary in a northerly direction (Wellhausen 1889:15) because the third side of the triangle is given when its three points are given. According to the description offered here Sodom, Gomorrah, Admah and Zeboim fall outside the territory of Canaan (cf Gitan 1984:639, who claims the opposite without argument). *boʾªkâ* (Qal participle of *bwʾ* with second person masculine singular suffix) must mean 'as you go' = 'in the direction of' because Gerar lies farther south than Gaza. Gaza is neither mentioned merely because it is better known than Gerar (so Simons 1948:91-117), nor a gloss (Gunkel, Procksch), nor is it the result of two traditions bluntly superimposed on one another (Westermann). To say that a straight line from Sidon via Gerar to Gaza is impossible because Gerar lies farther south-south-west, as Westermann does, is begging the question because the line is drawn from Sidon via Gaza to Gerar. Only the general direction is indicated.

As my thesis that Sodom and its associated cities were regarded as having been outside Canaan is not without importance for this study, the following is offered in support of it: Following Simons, Westermann claims without argument in an apparent reference to ʿad and boʾᵃkâ that the two 'prepositions' mean the same. In fact they are not always identical. Westermann quotes Genesius-Kautzsch, par 144h, which is not to the point because this paragraph is not about prepositional usage at all but only about the use of the second person masculine singular for the indefinite personal subject. We shall have to look at other instances where the two words are used. In Judges 6:4 ʿad boʾᵃkâ is used as one preposition meaning 'up to'; in Judges 11:33 ʿad boʾᵃkâ x as well as ʿad y occurs with the same meaning. Only in Genesis 10:30, where boʾᵃkâ occurs alone, does it mean 'up to the point of'. In Genesis 13:10, however, where boʾᵃkâ also stands alone, it cannot mean that because boʾᵃkâ ṣoʿar is the subject which follows the predicate in a nominal sentence; here it can only indicate general direction. In Genesis 10:19, which interests us here, we have neither boʾᵃkâ ʿad nor ʿad alone nor boʾᵃkâ alone, but first boʾᵃkâ x and then ʿad y (twice). The one therefore limits and defines the meaning of the other (a well-known phenomenon, cf Barr 1968:11-26). The same happens in Genesis 25:18, where the only difference is that ʿad x occurs first and boʾᵃkâ y second. This verse should then be translated: 'And they (the Ishmaelites) lived from Havilah to Shur at the entrance to Egypt, as you go towards Asshur'. Here ʿad means 'from one point up to another' and boʾᵃkâ must then indicate the general direction. The Arabian peninsula is clearly meant (as most commentators agree). 'The face of Egypt' must then indicate the northwestern part of this area, and Shur would be an Egyptian border point (Jacob) in the area where the road from Egypt to Assyria passes. Accordingly, a territory is described from one point to another (ʿad) and the general orientation (Arabia between Egypt and Assyria; boʾᵃkâ) is supplied as well. As far as I can see, this occurs three times, once in Genesis 25:18 and twice in Genesis 10:19.

Then Sodom and the other three cities must lie farther east than Lasha, which in turn would mean that the identification of the place with Callirrhoe on the eastern side of the Dead Sea (Targum Pseudo-Jonathan, BerR 37:6, and Jerome; cf Ginzberg 1900:90) is unsuitable (so also in the extensive treatment of the locality by Donner 1963:59-89). Whatever the location or the name of this place and however vague the description of the boundary may be, the four cities in question are not considered to be part of the land of Canaan (cf Von Rad, whose comment contradicts his translation).

In view of the awareness all over the Old Testament of the wickedness of Sodom and Gomorrah, it is almost surprising that our text refers neither to this motif nor to their destruction. However, I think that a negative evaluation of the cities is implied by our passage. The traditional cities of vice fall outside Canaan and are therefore not part of the Promised Land. The verse is usually allotted to the 'Jahwist Table'. It differs from the 'Priestly Table' in that it is not so rigidly structured as the latter and lacks the schematic priestly view of the world (cf Gunkel, Procksch, Skinner, Von Rad, Westermann). Accordingly, this view of Sodom and its associates should be placed in pre-exilic Judah, probably somewhat earlier than the author of the Sodom Cycle. Not only this text, but also Genesis 13:12 explicitly excludes Sodom and the other cities of the plain from Canaan (cf below). In view of the fact that Admah and Zeboim occur together in Hosea 11:8, where Sodom and Gomorrah are not mentioned, and that they occur together with the latter cities only in the post-exilic Deuteronomy 29:22 (as part of a group of four) and in the compounded Genesis 14 (as part of a group of five, the so-called 'Pentapolis'), Westermann is probably correct in judging that they have been added in the Table.

In **Genesis 13:10.12.13** Sodom and Gomorrah are mentioned without Admah and Zeboim. I have argued above that the story of Genesis 18-19 presupposes the events narrated in Genesis 13 (cf pp 42-43, 47). This does not necessarily mean, as Rudin-O'Brasky (who includes Gn 12) thinks, that Genesis 13.18-19 was one literary unit which had been taken apart by a redactor. The Sodom Cycle is too carefully balanced to be the product of mere redactional activity. While the literary unit in Genesis 18-19 can be read on its own and is not in need of an explanation of how Lot came to Sodom, the traditions underlying its material do require such an explanation. Genesis 13 shows that there was a tradition which supplied it. In verse 10a it is said that Lot saw that the Jordan valley was well watered. This can indeed be said of the valley before it reaches the Dead Sea, from which point southward just the opposite is true. So he chose the well watered valley (v 11a). Twice reference is made to the Jordan valley as *kol hakkikkâr*, the *whole* valley, not only the Dead Sea area. This fits several further statements in our text. First, Lot moves eastwards (v 11b) from the Bethel vicinity (vv 3.5). This would bring him into the Jordan valley at a point northeast of Jericho. Second, he goes to live (*yšb*) in the cities of the valley (v 12a; 'The verb *yšb* is not necessarily inconsistent with nomadic life' – Skinner, followed by Westermann). How did he reach Sodom? He 'tented towards Sodom' (*wayyè'ehal 'ad s'dom*), which means that he gradually moved his tents in the direction of Sodom until he eventually settled in the city. Westermann translates 'und zeltete bis hin nach Sodom', but appears to approve of Ginsberg's idea that the preposition *'ad* does not signify direction, but place (Ginsberg 1951:12-14). However, this is not supported by the examples he mentions (Gn 10:19, 13:12, 25:18

where not place, but direction is meant). In any case such a meaning would not suit our present context. We thus gather a picture of a nomadic Lot who gradually moved to a city. When we again meet him in Sodom (Gn 19) he has a house with a sturdy door and a beamed roof (cf Gn 19:6.8). It is important that verse 12 clearly counterpoises Canaan and the cities of the valley, specifically Sodom. Abram/Abraham remained in Canaan, while Lot left the Promised Land. This is understandable in the light of Genesis 19:30-38, where the ancestor of the Moabites and Ammonites, who was still in the region *boʾⁱkâ ṣoʿar*, fled to the hills on the eastern side of the valley, far from Canaan (cf above, pp 45-46). In view of the exclusion of Sodom and the valley-cities from Canaan, verses 10 and 12 reflect the same tradition as Genesis 10:19.

It is possible that the awkwardly formulated verse 10b contains two additions to verse 10a: 'Before Yahweh had destroyed Sodom and Gomorrah the region in the direction of Zoar (*boʾⁱkâ ṣoʿar*) was like the garden of Yahweh' + 'like the land of Egypt' (cf Dillmann; Westermann finds three additions). Nevertheless it reflects a different focus of interest from that of Genesis 18-19 and cannot, therefore, have been conceived under the influence of those chapters. Verse 10b interprets the reference to the well watered Jordan valley to include the area of Sodom and Gomorrah. Therefore it says that the good state of this area only prevailed before the destruction of the two cities and thus implies that the Sodom and Gomorrah area must lie farther south in the inhospitable Dead Sea region. The second possible addition may be the reference to Egypt, which looks like a gloss. However, it makes good sense in that it compares the fertility of Egypt, which depends on the Nile for its irrigation, with the Jordan valley which also depends on a river for its water. Verse 10b says that this was the case all the way to Zoar in the days before the destruction of the region. An important feature of the Judean tradition found here is therefore that the Sodom area was conceived of as having been paradise-like before it became desolate.

On the other hand verse 13 is obviously dependent on the story of Genesis 18-19. It follows the story in focussing on Sodom only. Moreover, the uncommon combination *ḥaṭṭâʾîm lyhwh* (Jacob) contains both the motif of the wickedness of the inhabitants and the motif of offence given to Yahweh, the God of Abraham.

Allowing for the focus of verse 13, these verses reflect the tradition that both Sodom and Gomorrah were destroyed. We must conclude that the older tradition spoke of Sodom and Gomorrah, while the author of the cycle drew from the tradition but only needed one city for his story. The Sodom Cycle itself is interested in something quite different from etiology, but these verses contain indications of etiological interest. The mentioning of the Jordan valley as a whole including the destroyed cities, and the attention given to the irrigational attractiveness of the region betray an underlying question: Why is the southern part of the valley so different from the northern part? The answer is that Yahweh destroyed the southern part. This, too, confirms our conclusion that an older tradition underlies the story of Genesis 19.

Genesis 14 is notorious for being one of the most controversial passages in the Pentateuch. Its notoriety stems from the impossibility of assigning it to the conventional sources used in Pentateuchal criticism (cf Procksch, who discusses the chapter in an 'Anhang' to his commentary) and from the fact that it contains 'in schreiendem Kontrast gut Beglaubigtes und ganz Unmögliches' (Gunkel). As we are only concerned with the Sodom and Gomorrah traditions, we shall only concentrate on those details that are relevant to our present interest (cf the survey given by Skinner and the detailed notes by Procksch).

Most commentators divide the chapter into broadly the same sections:

A. A report on a military campain (vv 1-11)
B. The rescue by Abram (vv 12-17.21-24)
C. Melchizedek and Abram (vv 18-20)

Verses 1-11 contain early elements in that these verses show similarity to the ancient royal inscriptions where we also find campaign reports of this kind (Westermann) and in that three of the royal names can be related to genuine Babylonian, Sumerian and Elamite proper names (cf Skinner). On the other hand there are also signs of artificiality. The names of the plain kings (not 'Canaanite' kings – cf Vawter) have alliterative effect: twice *bet* and twice *šin*. Moreover, the later Jewish exegesis is undoubtedly right in detecting puns on *ra'* (evil) and *rèša'* (wickedness) in the names of respectively *bèra'*, the king of Sodom and *birša'*, the king of Gomorrah (cf Ginzberg 1900:101-102, who also refers to Jerome, on Bela). Jacob is correct in this respect, although he was not the first to notice these artificialities (cf Skinner). He goes too far, however, in finding the whole chapter a disparagement of Sodom. Still, he rightly observes that the kings of Sodom and Gomorrah are the only ones who act. The other three kings of the Pentapolis (a name for the five cities of the plain occurring for the first time in Sap 10:6, cf below, p 78-79) seem to be left in mid-air; they participate in the revolt against Kedorlaomer, but we only hear about the kings of Sodom and Gomorrah (*ûmèlèk* to be read before *"morâ* in v 10) when the ignominious flight before the invaders is described. This is hardly coincidence and the picture conjured up by verse 10 is really ludicrous: The kings of Sodom and Gomorrah should know their vicinity, especially that there are dangerous bitumen pits on the terrain where the battle is fought. Yet not the foreigners, but the natives are the ones who are caught in the trap of their own land. What fools they look, wildly fleeing, not knowing their own land, and then tumbling into the pits. Van Hattem (1981:87) ignores this literary function of the kings' falling into the pits when he assumes that the (historical) kings would have known the territory and that the battle, which he dates between 2400 and 2300 BCE, must therefore have taken place farther afield. In this light it is not a problem that the king of Sodom appears alive again in verse 17. It is not said that he died, only that he and the king of Gomorrah are a pathetic bunch. For these reasons we can agree with Gunkel that this passage reflects a late post-exilic tradition. It is true, as Westermann objects, that Abram does not appear in this section and that his presence would match other post-exilic texts (such as Judith) where a Jewish saviour features. This is of course the case from the perspective of the redactor who added the sections of the chapter together (which Westermann himself contends), but even without this perspective the first section by itself fits well into the post-exilic period where we often find artificial names and where kings often appear as ignoramuses and fools (cf the artificial names in Dn 1:7, 3:12 etc and in Est 1:10.14; also the figures of Nebuchadnezzar and Darius in the Book of Daniel and Xerxes in the Book of Esther).

Verses 12-17.21-24 contain a story of liberation. Emerton (1971b, cf also 1971a) has the credit of recognising that this section is to be considered against the backdrop of the stories of the Judges (cf also 1 Sm 30, which dates from roughly the same period). We find Abram as a hero (cf Emerton 1971b:431-433) who acts in the typical pattern of the Judges. A foreign power invades the land and makes off with booty; then a local leader appears, rallies support, overpowers the invader and restores the situation. Emerton compares Abram's 318 men with Gideon's 300 (Jdg 7:7) and Abram's magnanimity (vv 22-24) with that of Gideon (Jdg 8:23). To this we can also add the remark by Westermann that the problem of whether the liberator may establish himself as a power in his own right was topical in the time of the Judges. All of this shows convincingly that this section hails from the period of the Judges and is therefore a story of a typical Judge who has been identified with the patriarch Abram/Abraham. The king of Sodom, who is the only one of the Pentapolis kings to feature in this section, does not appear in a particularly bad light (v 21). Offering the goods to Abram may imply that he considers himself to have the right to give away what now in fact is already Abram's, but this is unlikely (in the Genesis Apocryphon from Qumran, col 22, l 18, the king of Sodom even addresses Abram as 'my lord' (*mârî 'abrâm*) and therefore acknowledges Abram's superiority). The point is that Abram dissociates himself from the king of Sodom. Thus it cannot be said that the father of Israel has even indirectly had a part in the prosperity of the evil city.

In verses 18-20, where Sodom and Gomorrah are not mentioned, the Jerusalem cult is legitimated. The passage should therefore be dated in the early monarchy. From a redactional point of view we may say that these verses form a contrast to verses 22-24 in that Abram's humility towards Melchizedek throws his pride towards the king of Sodom into sharper relief (cf Von Rad).

This is the only text in the Old Testament where the five cities of the Pentapolis feature together. Vawter (1977:192) has noticed that the interest in these cities narrows down in the course of the chapter from all five to the twosome of Sodom and Gomorrah, and ultimately to Sodom alone. This reflects their positions in the Sodom and Gomorrah traditions generally. In the centre is Sodom; second, if only because of being mentioned often together with Sodom, comes Gomorrah; then comes Zoar, which has a special role as Lot's refuge; and on the periphery come Admah and Zeboim, who will take centre stage in Hosea 11:8 (cf below, pp 67-69). This relationship of the cities of the Pentapolis to one another has not been noticed by Van Selms who, curiously, offers an excursus on the Pentapolis at Genesis 19 instead of Genesis 14. He reckons only with four of the five cities and claims that the outstanding feature in these traditions is always the irrigation issue. Neither of these views is correct in respect of Genesis 14, which fact is probably to be ascribed to the place in the commentary where the matter is considered.

Let us sum up briefly our conclusions about the predominant motifs of the Sodom and Gomorrah traditions in Genesis, apart from the Sodom Cycle itself:

1. In the time of the Judges the Sodom tradition was already associated with the Abraham tradition in such a way that Abraham, a typical southern sheikh, was presented as the proud military superior of the king of Sodom and economically independent of him.

2. During the middle period of the monarchy, earlier than the seventh century, the Judean tradition regarded Sodom and her associates as not having been part of Canaan – a geographic dissociation in keeping with the economic dissociation of the period of the Judges.

3. During the same period Sodom and the other cities of the valley were regarded to have been a well watered, paradise-like region which had been made desolate by Yahweh during the time of the patriarchs.

4. The motif of their utter offensiveness to Yahweh was maintained after the seventh century under the influence of the Sodom Cycle.

5. In late post-exilic times the tradition of the evil Sodom and Gomorrah was used to ridicule foreign kings in a manner typical of post-exilic Jewish literature.

3.2. The other books of the Hebrew Old Testament

Outside of Genesis Sodom and Gomorrah (usually together, twice Sodom alone, and once both together with Admah and Zeboim) occur in two texts from Deuteronomy, one from Lamentations and predominantly in the southern prophets. The tradition is found in one northern prophet, Hosea (if we count Amos as a southerner), but there only Admah and Zeboim feature. It should also be noticed that the list of occurrences drawn up by Westermann (1981:363) is not accurate and contains several mistakes and omissions. One of the Deuteronomic passages is cited twice according to the verse numbering of a translation instead of according to the Hebrew Bible (Dt 29:23 should read 29:22); later the same text is erroneously cited as Dt 19:22. Furthermore, three occurrences of either Sodom and Gomorrah or Sodom alone are missing from the list, viz Deuteronomy 32:32, Isaiah 3:9 and Jeremiah 23:14. Finally, Psalm 11:6 is in the list, but none of the cities in question are mentioned there; at most one may find an indirect allusion to the tradition in the verse (Schlosser 1973:14 calls it an 'implicit citation' of Gn 19:24).

Deuteronomy 29:22 is interesting as it forms part of the so-called Covenant of the Plains of Moab (cf already Driver, although he uses different terminology, viz 'Moses' Third Discourse' and 'Deuteronomic Covenant'). It is not the easiest of texts to analyse, but for our purpose we need not get involved in the detailed arguments concerning the whole passage (Dt 28:69 - 29:28). Even though Preuss (1982:158) is undoubtedly right in judging that Von Rad's presentation of the chapter is somewhat simplistic, we may follow the latter in measuring the passage according to the sections of the Covenant Formulary (cf Baltzer 1964:20, whose summary of the sections of the 'Bundesformular' differs from that given in Von Rad's summary of Dt 29-30, e.g. the inversion of the last two elements; there are, however, examples of the order found in our text, cf Goetze 1955:205). First comes the preamble (Dt 29:1-7), then the declaration of principle (Dt 29:8), blessings and curses (Dt 30:16-18), and finally the mentioning of witnesses (Dt 30:19-20). Inbetween diverse material has been inserted. Our text is part of such a homiletic expansion (cf Lohfink 1962:40-41) or parenthesis. By referring to the past, the section gives a vivid picture of what can be expected in the future, and in so doing reference is made to the Sodom tradition. If Yahweh's people turn away from him, it means that they have broken the Covenant. Then he himself will reject them and the result will be exile 'as it is today' (v 27). The four cities of the plain were also devastated by Yahweh. Burning sulphur (cf Gn 19:24) and salt (cf Gn 19:26) will again be a feature of the land like in the time of Sodom, Gomorrah, Admah and Zeboim. If not exactly a formal curse, this is a threat which may reflect a traditional curse in which Sodom and Gomorrah featured (Hillers 1964:74-75).

Weinfeld (1972:111) refers to some of the prophetic Sodom and Gomorrah texts (cf below) and contends that they 'occur in connection with breach of treaty'. Therefore he finds it legitimate to assume 'that the overthrow of Sodom and Gomorrah was conceived as the classic punishment of breach of covenant with the Deity'. He is correct in comparing the wasteland of the Sodom tradition to what we find in this text as well as in other treaty-type texts from the Ancient Near East (Weinfeld 1972:109-112). But it does not follow that Sodom and Gomorrah were conceived of as having broken a covenant with Yahweh (Weinfeld does not say, 'an overthrow *like* that of Sodom and Gomorrah'). In fact, this would be rather a strange idea for the deuteronomic-deuteronomistic current of thinking. There has to be a covenant if it is to be broken, and a covenant between Yahweh and the people of Sodom and her sister cities would be difficult to imagine. However, we may turn Weinfeld's idea (covenant - punishment) around and conclude that the classic illustration of punishment for offending the deity, contained in the Sodom and Gomorrah tradition, was applied to the breaking of the covenant of Yahweh (punishment - covenant). This was facilitated by the fact that the motif of laying waste the land of the offenders and making it salt occurred both in the Sodom and Gomorrah tradition and often in the treaty literature of the Ancient Near East. However, Jerusalem was not devastated in the same way as Sodom and Gomorrah. As the exile is presupposed here (v 27) we will also have to conclude that the focus falls on only one aspect of the punishment of Sodom and Gomorrah. The *tertium comparationis* is not that Yahweh brought/will bring fiery rain from heaven, but that a wasteland *results* from his punishment. The reference to Sodom and its sister cities serves a function in our exilic text which runs remarkably parallel to what we have found the function of the Sodom Cycle itself to be. Perlitt (1969:23) places our chapter in an early exilic theological 'Herausarbeitung der Schuld Israels in Korrespondenz zur Entschuldigung Jahwes'. This is basically what I have said earlier of the Sodom story in Genesis 18-19 (cf above, p 46-47): Wickedness of humans is punished, but not at the cost of Yahweh becoming unjust himself.

Deuteronomy 32:32, one of the occurrences omitted by Westermann, is interesting because of its imagery and because of the fact that it reflects on the wickedness of nations other than Israel. In verses 26-35 we have a self-consultation of Yahweh (*'âmartî*, 'I thought by myself' – Von Rad). Yahweh had thought earlier that he should have exterminated Israel completely, but he refrained from doing so because of the danger of the enemies of Israel ascribing her downfall to their own strength. These nations are now compared to a vine. Their vine derives from the vine of Sodom, or, in the parallel hemistich, it is a product from the fields of Gomorrah. The first element of tradition to be observed here is the motif of the agricultural paradise which the Sodom and Gomorrah vicinity was believed to have been prior to the disaster. What is now a wasteland, previously produced grapes (cf, for the motif of Sodom's fruit, Sap 10:7 and p 78 below). However, these are perverted into the opposite of what one would expect a paradise to produce. Even before the destruction the fruit of Sodom and Gomorrah was poisonous and bad. This is of course possible in a poem where the motif is used metaphorically. Secondly, it means that the wickedness of the nations is innate (cf Driver), a characteristic of the 'Sodom cultivar' that cannot be changed. In this passage Sodom and Gomorrah are, then, rather symbols of wickedness than of destruction. This fits well into the exilic period where the question of Yahweh's power *vis-à-vis* the other gods and the wickedness of those who had trampled on Israel is understandable. In addition, this kind of 'last words' literature is typical of the post-exilic period, while verse 21 presupposes the destruction of Judah (Fohrer 1965:206) so that we cannot follow Weiser (1966:110) and others (cf Hillers 1964:75) in assigning a very early date to the Song of Moses.

Isaiah 1:9.10 contain two separate references to Sodom and Gomorrah belonging to two separate passages in the chapter. The 'arch-structure' found by Watts in Isaiah 1:2-23 is not convincing since the 'parallel thoughts' in the supposedly corresponding sections (vv 2//21-23, 3//18-20, 4-5//15b-17, 6-7b//10-15a; 'keystone': vv 7c-9) are too vague. As Wildberger points out, the division of sections between verses 9 and 10 is marked by the introductory appeal in verse 10 (the imperative *šim'û*). This is not weakened by the fact that Sodom and Gomorrah are mentioned in both verse 9 and verse 10, because that is the reason why the two sections have been placed alongside each other.

After the exclamation of woe in verse 4 the sins and subsequent hardship of the Judeans are introduced. They have forsaken Yahweh (v 4) and have been smitten as a consequence (v 6). Part of this misfortune consists of the land and its cities having been made desolate (*š'mâmâ*) and burnt with fire (*š'rupôt 'eš*, v 7). There is only one exception: Jerusalem (*bat* ṣiyyôn) has been left over (nôtᵉrâ, v 8) like a booth in a vineyard or in a field of cucumbers. The imagery is clear: Only Jerusalem stands, while the rest of the land has been ravaged. Kaiser is correct that we know nothing of a destruction of Jerusalem in 701 BCE, but this does not argue against dating the passage somewhat after this time, because the devastation of the country and the bare survival of Jerusalem after the campaign by Sennacherib in 701 BCE (cf Oppenheim 1955:287-288) fit the picture painted in our passage admirably. Verse 9 connects the Isaianic idea of the 'remnant' with the tradition of Sodom and Gomorrah. Had Yahweh not left a remnant of his people, they would have become like Sodom and Gomorrah, that is, they would have been completely wiped out (not 'almost', as contended by Watts, whose reading of kim'aṭ with this meaning and after the verse divider does not remedy a supposed 'awkward sense', but creates one; they are 'almost' wiped out as it is; cf Van Uchelen 1981:158, who also reads kim'aṭ in the apodosis, but as an intensifying conjunction). Watts thinks that 'the comparison to Sodom and Gomorrah does not quite fit', which should probably be attributed to his faulty reading of kim'aṭ and his division of verse 9. Wildberger also finds the comparison surprising because Sodom and Gomorrah were not destroyed by military means. However, this need not surprise us because the *tertium comparationis* is again, as in the case of Deuteronomy 29:22, the final state of Sodom and Gomorrah, not the way in which they were destroyed. Whether we regard the verse as the rejection of a prophetic indictment in verses 2-8 (Van Uchelen 1981:161-163) or as a reference to the bare survival of Jerusalem in a devastated land, the function of the Sodom and Gomorrah tradition remains the same.

The opening verse of the second passage in question (Is 1:10-17) speaks of Sodom and Gomorrah in parallelism. Here the moot point is whether sacrifice is rejected in principle, which is not our immediate concern in this study (cf the discussion by Kaiser). What does concern us is that the leaders as well as the common people are addressed. 'Leaders of Sodom' and 'people of Gomorrah' are used in synonymous parallelism so that the two cities become one in function (cf Zeph 2:9, where Sodom and Gomorrah are also split in parallelism but one in function). The passage severely reprimands the whole cultic community for accompanying their external piety with injustice. Therefore we are justified in saying that their wickedness in general is scathed by calling them by the names of the classic examples of iniquity (cf the first century MartIs 3:10, where this dictum of Isaiah is used as evidence against him by his adversary, Belchira – which shows that Is 1:10 was likewise understood as very harsh words in the first century). We are not justified, however, in following Wildberger's pure guesswork about the existence of a tradition according to which the people of Sodom and Gomorrah were active in pious cultic practices but inactive in social justice. Because of the cult criticism and its reminiscences of Amos (cf Am 3:14, 4:4-5, 5:21-27) we can date this prophecy in the time of Isaiah.

Isaiah 3:9 contains a gloss *kisdom* which makes the verse awkwardly long and metrically improbable (cf Duhm, Wildberger, Kaiser). For this reason it is probably late exilic. It reflects the tradition of Sodom's injustice in judgement, for it is added to a pronouncement about just this form of injustice in Jerusalem (*hakkârat pᵉnêhèm*, 'favouritism'). This is found in later Jewish traditions (cf pp 111-116). It is possible that we here have the first instance of this specific form of wickedness associated with Sodom.

In **Isaiah 13:19** (and vv 20-22) we find a passage which is particularly germane to the thesis of Hillers (1964:53, 75-76) that the mentioning of Sodom and Gomorrah in prophetic references to sudden destruction should be explained in terms of a traditional curse. Babylon is threatened with destruction like that of Sodom and Gomorrah. Watts has made out a convincing case that this, though surprising in the eighth century, can be dated in the time of Ahaz (1985:188, 200). 'At this time Babylon was the prime symbol of successful revolt against Assyrian sovereignty.' As Assyria was still Yahweh's rod, rebellion like that of Babylon 'by any of the small nations would be futile and, worse, it would be rebellion against God'. Because of her revolt against the rod of God, and therefore her bad example to Israel, Babylon is solemnly cursed (cf the solemn expression *'ad dôr wâdôr* in v 20 and the poetic picture of the wild animals who will inhabit the city) to undergo the fate of the classic types of God's wrath. The fact that *'ᵉlohîm* and not *yhwh* is used here, is attributed by Kraetschmar (1897:87-88) to the fact that the phrase *mahpekat 'ᵉlohîm 'èt sᵉdom wᵉ'èt 'ᵃmorâ* was a fixed formula (cf below, pp 65-66 on Am 4:11).

Wildberger makes a remark in his discussion of Isaiah 1:4-9 (1972:30) which deserves our attention. He ascribes the knowledge of the pre-exilic prophets (Isaiah, Amos, Zephaniah, Jeremiah, Ezekiel, and the northerner Hosea) about Sodom and Gomorrah to the fact that these cities were also known in the covenant tradition ('Bundestradition') with which these prophets were familiar. This is certainly a possibility made attractive by what we have seen above (pp 56-57 about the relationship between the Sodom and Gomorrah tradition and the covenant tradition). On the other hand too much should not be made of the differences between this covenant/prophetic tradition and the Sodom Cycle in Genesis 18-19. Wildberger expresses the suspicion that the two complexes are fundamentally ('wesentlich') different, which is just the opposite of Kaiser's opinion. According to Wildberger the fact that *mahpekâ* is 'constantly' used in the covenant tradition (Dt 29:22, the emended text of Is 1:7 where *kᵉmahpekat sᵉdom* is read instead of *kᵉmahpekat zârîm*, Is 13:19, Am 4:11, Jr 49:18, 50:40) shows that we have a different version of the Sodom and Gomorrah tradition before us. This argument is substantially devalued by the fact that the same root occurs several times in de Sodom Cycle (*hᵃpekâ* in Gn 19:29, *hpk* in Gn 19:21.25.29). Moreover, Wildberger claims that an earthquake is suggested by *mahpekâ* and implies that this differs from what we find in Genesis 19. In fact this is not at variance with the story (cf above, p 40-41). So we conclude that the Sodom and Gomorrah tradition found in Isaiah is similar to that found in other pre-exilic prophets and in the covenant tradition, but that its motifs are not fundamentally different from or irreconcilable with the narrative in Genesis 19. The function of the use of the tradition in the book is twofold: To show that the sins of Judah/Israel are as bad as those of the classic examples of vice (Is 1:10, 3:9), and to dramatise the total destruction to which Jerusalem had come near (Is 1:9) and to which Babylon was approaching (Is 13:19).

Turning to the Book of Jeremiah, we find three references to Sodom and Gomorrah and one allusion to the cities (Jr 20:16). The first reference is **Jeremiah 23:14.** It is part of a passage usually demarcated as verses 13-15 (cf Rudolph, Carroll, Holladay) which consists of a comparison between the prophets of Samaria (v 13) and the prophets of Jerusalem (v 14), as well as an announcement of judgement (v 15). The comparison is to the detriment of the prophets of Jerusalem. The Samarian prophets did 'an unsavoury thing' (Carroll's translation of *tiplâ*), but the Jerusalem prophets committed horrible things (*šaᶜᵃrûrâ*). Whereas the former group caused Israel to apostatise after Baal, the latter group committed adultery and lies and strengthened the position of the evildoers. Their offence is moral, and moral offence is worse than cultic offence – a typical Jeremianic idea. This is why the prophets of Jerusalem are likened to the people of Sodom and the inhabitants of the city (who follow the guidance of their prophets) to the people of Gomorrah. The parallelism of the cities and the matching parallelism between a leading group in Jerusalem and the general populace is also found in Isaiah 1:10. Adultery and general wickedness accord well with the picture of the evil city in Genesis 19. Here the function of the Sodom and Gomorrah tradition is to typify the wickedness of the prophets and inhabitants of Jerusalem.

Two closely related passages are to be found in **Jeremiah 49:18 and 50:40.** In both cases we have prophecies against other nations, Edom in the first and Babylon in the second. Jeremiah 49:12-22 consists mostly of later expansions as suggested by the 'generality of reference which permits them to be used interchangeably' (Carroll). Part of this is verse 18 where Sodom and Gomorrah appear in the familiar expression k^emahpekat s^edom wa^{ca}morâ, this time followed by uš^{e}kenèhâ, 'and her neighbours' (i e Admah and Zeboim, cf Gn 10:19, Gn 14, Dt 29:22). The second main function of the Sodom and Gomorrah tradition is thus again in evidence: The cities are the classic examples of total destruction. The same is the case in Jeremiah 50:40, where the neighbouring cities are mentioned again, but where ^{ve}lohîm is used instead of yahweh (another difference is that the nota accusativi is used here, but not in Jr 49:18). As in the previous chapter and in Isaiah 13:19, the desolation is complete and vividly described by the use of animal images (albeit somewhat differently in Jr 49:19, but cf Jr 49:19-21 and 50:44-46). The fate of Babylon is described with such close similarity to Isaiah 13:19 that Rudolph thinks it has been drawn from the earlier passage and that Jeremiah 49:18 shares in the dependence. It is possible that he is right in both instances (cf Carroll on the date of Jr 50: the grandiloquence and the insignificance of the actual changeover of power between the Babylonians and the Persians point to a date after 539 BCE). The context in Jeremiah 50 contains another interesting parallel to the Sodom and Gomorrah tradition: In verse 38 a drought is announced over the waters of Babylon. The well watered land will become a wasteland. This is an established motif in the Sodom and Gomorrah tradition (cf Gn 13; above, p 52).

Ezekiel 16:44-58 is perhaps, with the possible exception of Hosea 11:8 (cf below, pp 67-69), the most noteworthy of the prophetic references to Sodom. The passage is usually demarcated as I have done (cf Fohrer, Zimmerli), and even if it is taken to be part of a larger unit a caesura is often indicated after verse 58 (cf Wevers, Brownlee 1986:242). Jerusalem first features as the daughter of her mother and the sister of her sisters (vv 44-46; cf also Ezk 23, where two cities are sisters with names); then follows an extended comparison to her sisters, of which Sodom is by far the most prominent (vv 47-50 + 51); next come an injunction (v 52), the restoration of the three sisters (vv 53-55), and finally a conclusion about the disgrace of Jerusalem (vv 56-58).

The focus of our attention is, of course, drawn to the comparison between Jerusalem and Sodom. Gomorrah is not mentioned at all, but Sodom's neighbours are included by the addition of ûb^{e}nôtèhâ, 'and her daughters', an ancient expression to indicate lesser neighbouring towns (cf Jdg 1:27, Zimmerli). Samaria also has such dependent towns, as does Jerusalem (v 48). Sodom is the smaller sister, since the politically more prominent Samaria has to be the 'big' sister. However, in this passage Sodom has a more prominent role than Samaria (cf vv 48-50/51). The sisters can be expected to be wicked because their mother was a bad wife to her husband and a bad mother to her children. Sodom's sin was that it combined a luxurious life with insolence and social oppression (vv 49-50). Then comes the most offensive thing that could be said of Jerusalem: Her wickedness is worse than that of Samaria who has been destroyed because of her sins and, horror of horrors, she even surpasses the wickedness of Sodom, the example *par excellence* of depravity and total destruction (v 50). So both the aspects of the Sodom symbolism are found here – Sodom as the type of wickedness and as the arch-example of the destructive wrath of God. This is succinctly formulated by Neher (1979:484) when he says that Sodom is 'l'incarnation même de la mort morale et physique'. Accordingly Jerusalem can expect to undergo the same treatment as her sisters. However, the second surprise of the passage is found at this juncture. The punishment of total destruction is not worked out; Jerusalem will have to bear her shame as her sisters had to do earlier (vv 52.54.57.58), but she is not threatened with total demolition. This is unexpected and must have a good reason. At least two equally unexpected statements are made in the context. First, Jerusalem is said to have interceded for her sisters and to have made them 'righteous' (*pillalt la'ᵃḥôtek, ṣaddèqtek 'aḥyôtek*, v 52). Second, she is said to have been a consolation to them (*naḥᵃmek 'otân*, v 54). Each of these statements is accompanied by the motif of Jerusalem's shame (twice in v 52 and once in v 54). Therefore the shame of Jerusalem must have something to do with the consolation of Sodom and Samaria. What this entails is given in verses 53 and 55: All three of the sisters are to be restored to their former glory. In this sense Jerusalem interceded for her sisters by her shameful wickedness: If Yahweh wishes to restore Jerusalem, then he must also restore Sodom and Samaria since their wickedness was less than that of Jerusalem. Ezekiel thus appears as the vindicator of Sodom, and as such occupies a unique position in almost the whole Sodom and Gomorrah tradition. Not even the relative preference of Sodom and Gomorrah in some New Testament passages and in the Wisdom of Solomon goes as far as this (cf Mt 10:15, 11:23.24, Lk 10:12, Sap 19:14-17). As far as I can see, the idea of a restitution of Sodom occurs, apart from Ezekiel, only in Tanchuma Genesis 47b; Aphraates as well as Jerome knew that some Jews thought so (Ginzberg 1900:110); Jerome, however, criticises them for this.

The impact of the idea of Sodom's restoration can be highlighted by considering two other elements of the Sodom tradition with reference to Ezekiel. The first is developed at length by Neher (1979:483-490). According to him Abraham, who is mentioned in a passage (Ezk 33:24) which is related to another (Ezk 11:14) where Ezekiel assumes the role of *go'el* of his people, was an unsuccessful redeemer of Sodom since his 'prayer' ('prière') for Sodom was not 'heard' ('ecoutée'). Therefore Ezekiel becomes the successful redeemer and thus achieves what even Abraham could not achieve. In my opinion this is going too far. If we consider that Abraham is only mentioned once in the book and that an indirect relationship is to be construed between that text (Ezk 33:24) and another (Ezk 11:14), the precarious basis for such a far-reaching conclusion becomes obvious. It is possible, however, to say that Ezekiel's view of the restoration of Sodom goes beyond the concern of the author of Genesis 18:17-33 without ascribing such a sweeping function to the figure of Abraham. In view of the fact that our passage in Ezekiel quotes from the Sodom Cycle (see below), it can be argued that Ezekiel developed the complex of motifs in the story to suit his own requirements, from (as he understood it):

wickedness - 'intercession' - 'failure' - destruction

to:

wickedness - worse wickedness - acquittal - restoration

Yahweh's desire to restore Jerusalem requires that the other cities be restored also, and Jerusalem has to bear her shame at the thought that she is the most sinful of all.

The second aspect in support of the importance of Sodom's restoration for Ezekiel is to be found in the description of the temple river and the boundaries of the land (Ezk 47, shortly referred to by Neher 1979:490). Here we encounter the motifs of the paradise-like land (vv 1-12, cf above, p 52) and the borderline of the southeastern corner of the land (vv 18.19, cf p 49). Ezekiel pictured the river springing from the altar as lifegiving, coming as it does from the presence of God and therefore resembling the river of Paradise (Gn 2:10, cf Fohrer 1955:245). It flows eastward and down the Jordan valley in a southerly direction to reach the Dead Sea which will be 'healed' (v 8) with the exception of a few holes from which a supply of salt will be available (v 11). Plant and fish life will flourish and the whole region will be 'healed' or restored (vv 7.9). This is clearly part of the same pattern of ideas as those that we have been considering. The Dead Sea vicinity, which is desolate and salty, is to become the paradise that it was (cf Gn 13:10). The Sodom region is to be restored together with her sister Jerusalem as is said several times in Ezekiel 16, and now the worst of the sisters is to become the fountainhead of the other's restoration. Moreover, all of this is also supported by Ezekiel's description of the boundaries of the new, healed land. Whereas Genesis 10:19 *excludes* the Sodom and Gomorrah region from the land, Ezekiel *includes* this region. The eastern boundary reaches right down to the Dead Sea (Ezk 47:18); then the line proceeds farther south and west to the Mediterranean (v 19), so the traditional Sodom and Gomorrah area is clearly incorporated. I would maintain that this lends extra support to my argument on Genesis 10:19. The idea of restoration itself means that a new situation arises; consequently the incorporation of the Sodom area as part of the new dispensation makes sense if it was excluded from the land under the old dispensation.

Ezekiel's higly original view of Sodom under the theme of 'Paradise lost' and 'Paradise regained' does not mean that he stood in a different line of tradition. On the contrary, we have seen that he received the traditional motifs that we have been studying earlier on and that he gave them an original *interpretation*. This is also apparent in Ezekiel 16:50, where Genesis 18:20 is interpreted (Yahweh sees the wickedness, *r'h* in both cases, before he does something about it; cf Brownlee). It is also evident from the dependence of Ezekiel's restoration motif on the dialogue between Abraham and Yahweh (while the latter is about the question whether Sodom can be saved because of the *innocence* of some people, the former is about the restoration of Sodom because of the *guilt* of others). This in turn supports my date for the Sodom Cycle, which must be earlier than Ezekiel (cf p 46-47). Therefore Zimmerli's question (also asked by others, cf Schlosser 1973:19) about the description of Sodom's sins in verse 49 can also be answered. The gluttony, complacency and social irresponsibility should not be ascribed to a variant tradition as opposed to a 'mainline' tradition about the sexual sins depicted in Genesis 19. Ezekiel's view is not even much of an adaptation, which arose from social conditions in Israel, of the wickedness motif found in Genesis 18-19, although the social *focus* of the prophecy is in keeping with these conditions. Ezekiel's social motif is essentially the same as that of the Sodom Cycle. For, as Brownlee argues, the sexual violence of the Sodomites is also a form of social violence or oppression.

In conclusion we can say that Sodom still features as the symbol of wickedness and destruction in spite of Ezekiel's restoration ideas because it is still the yardstick – if anyone is worse than Sodom, then he or she is *the* worst. But also: If Sodom can be restored to glory, then anyone can.

Our next prophetic reference is **Amos 4:11.** There is widespread agreement that the verse is part of a clearly structured passage in Amos 4:4-13 (cf Wolff, Rudolph, Brueggemann 1965:1-15), while the relationship of verses 4-5 and 6-13 is disputed (Amsler sees them as independent but in judicious contrast to each other and Wolff dates vv 6-13 in the time of Josiah). The debate is not central to our interest and we may concentrate on the position of Sodom and Gomorrah in the rigidly built up section vv 6-13. There are five units in the *catalogus calamitatum*, as Rudolph calls it, each devoted to a plague (v 6 - hunger, vv 7.8 - drought, v 9 - crop disease, v 10 - pestilence, v 11 - a catastrophe like that of Sodom and Gomorrah), and a conclusion (vv 12-13). At the end of each unit it is regularly said that Israel remained unrepentant. This means that the plagues were meant to bring about repentance. Even the climax of the visitations by Yahweh, the demolition by a *mahpekâ*, failed to bring them to repentance. Therefore they are to prepare to be confronted directly with him (v 12).

The 'Sodom and Gomorrah formula' (*k^{e}mahpekat $^{\gamma e}$lohîm 'èt s^{e}dom w^{e}'èt ^{ca}morâ*) contains the only reference to $^{\gamma e}$*lohîm* in Amos who regularly uses the name *yhwh* (cf Is 13:19, Jr 50:40, where the word $^{\gamma e}$*lohîm* also occurs). This is the clearest indication of the independence of the expression as an established formula (cf already Kraetschmar 1897:87-88). It may reflect the two stages with which we have occupied ourselves extensively in our study of Genesis 18-19, an early polytheistic view of the destruction of the cities and a later Yahwistic perspective which took over the old tradition (so Kraetschmar 1897:88, Rudolph). Wolff takes *mahpekâ* to refer to the political demise of the Northern Kingdom in 721 BCE, claiming that the formula always means political destruction. This is not the case, for, as we have seen several times, the condition of the land, its barrenness and the unsuitability for human inhabitation is always meant (cf Rudolph). The natural interpretation of *mahpekâ* as an earthquake is not only compatible with Genesis 19, where *hpk* occurs several times (vv 21.25.29) and where the context *can* be interpreted as referring to an earthquake (which Wolff denies without argument; cf Wildberger on Is 1:4-9, pp 58-59 above), but it is also compatible with Amos 1:1 where we hear of an earthquake which followed Amos's activity; the two earthquakes need not be the same (earth tremors are not rare in the country - Rudolph).

Brueggemann (1965:1-15) claims that verses 4-13 form a 'liturgy of covenant renewal' and that, accordingly, our passage consists of a series of 'covenant curses'. However, the references to what Yahweh has done in the past can hardly be seen as curses. The resemblance of some of the motifs in our passage to some motifs in Leviticus 26 does not prove that Amos celebrated a covenant renewal. So Weinfeld (1972:111; cf above, p 57) is not justified in stating on Brueggemann's authority that our passage occurs 'in connection with breach of treaty'. Again Sodom and Gomorrah are the symbols of destruction, and as such stand at the pinnacle of a list of catastrophes. If Israel remained unrepentant even after such a castigation, it cannot be imagined what will bring them to repentance.

In **Zephaniah 2:9** we have a prophecy against Moab and Ammon, embedded in an oracle stretching from verse 8 to the end of verse 11, which in turn is part of a context of oracles against different nations. In the parallelism Moab is likened to Sodom and Ammon to Gomorrah, which means both become like the sister cities of the Dead Sea plain (cf Is 1:10, where the two are also split in the parallelism but one in function). They will become desolate because of their haughtiness against Israel (v 10). The remark probably refers to an event such as described in 2 Kings 24:2, where we hear about raids by these two nations against Judah which took place about 602 BCE (Horst). This fits in well with the period of Zephaniah's activity. The prophecy against Moab and Ammon uses Sodom and Gomorrah as symbols of devastation in the same vein as the oracle Babylon in Isaiah 13:19-22. However, no allusion is made to the last passage of the Sodom Cycle, where Moab and Ammon are prominent (Gn 19:30-38). Although an *argumentum e silentio* is not conclusive proof, we may look upon this as a sign of the existence of Sodom and Gomorrah traditions that were not dependent on the story of Genesis 18-19. Two other pointers in this direction are the use of *ᵓelohîm* instead of *yhwh* (cf p 66) and the occurrence of Gomorrah in all but two references to Sodom (the exceptions are Is 3:9 and Lm 4:6; cf also Hs 11:8). Together with these, our text in Zephaniah 2:9 suggests that a tradition about the cities of Sodom and Gomorrah existed in which no mention was made of Israel's two eastern neighbours and in which 'the gods' featured. This tradition was the source on which the Genesis story as well as the prophets and other users of the theme drew (cf below, p 68-69).

Hosea 11:8 is the only text in the Old Testament where Admah and Zeboim occur together without Sodom and Gomorrah. The verse is part of a passage that is usually regarded as a unity (Hs 11:1-11; cf Wolff and Rudolph, but on the other hand Robinson who thinks that the chapter consists of four units). The passage begins with Ephraim's blindness to Yahweh's love (vv 1-4), the faithlessness of the people and its consequence (vv 5-7), Yahweh's change of mind and its consequence (vv 8-11). There are several problems with the text of the passage (cf the extensive notes given by Wolff and Rudolph), but none of these affect our interpretation of verse 8 directly. The verse is structured in a precise parallelism. By means of a rhetorical question (cf Gn 39:9, 44:34, Jr 9:6, Ps 137:4 for *ᵓêk*, which is not the same as the cry of lament; so Rudolph, rejecting Robinson's view) Yahweh says that he can neither surrender Ephraim/Israel nor make them like Admah and Zeboim. Elsewhere these two towns only occur in Genesis 10:19, 14:2.8 and Deuteronomy 29:22 and, because of their exclusive association with Sodom and Gomorrah, obviously represent that tradition. They are again symbols of devastation, but not of wickedness. The sin of Ephraim in this context is idolatry (v 2), although the social dimension is not absent elsewhere in the book (cf Hs 7:1, 12:9). But, as in Ezekiel 16, another dimension is added which makes the use of the Sodom and Gomorrah tradition very interesting. According to the implication of the rhetorical question Yahweh ought to destroy Ephraim as completely as he had destroyed Admah and Zeboim. This is indeed what Israel is threatened with in Hosea 9:6, 10:7.8.14, where the idea of destruction and a wasteland is present. But now Yahweh cannot bring himself to do to Ephraim what he had done to Admah and Zeboim. This is developed further by the highly suggestive use of *hpk*. This root is used in Deuteronomy 29, where the two cities are mentioned by name, and also in Genesis 19:21.25.29. This is scarcely coincidence. What Hosea is saying, is that Yahweh takes the *mahpekâ* upon himself; instead of overturning Ephraim, his own heart is overturned. Wolff finds this an example of Hosea's God who struggles with himself on Israel's behalf. In his discussion of Genesis 18:20-33 Von Rad also refers to Hosea 11:8 and is followed by Brueggemann (1982:173) who asserts that Yahweh does here only what Abraham had asked of him, viz to act like God and not like man (cf Gn 18:25 and Hs 11:9 - *'el 'ânokî wᵉlô' 'îš*). It is obvious that Yahweh intends not to destroy, but to save. In this regard the use of the Sodom and Gomorrah tradition (or the Admah and Zeboim tradition) is comparable to the use made of it in Ezekiel 16. Although no mention is made of the restoration of the ancient cities (cf Ezk 16:53), the fundamental tendency of the two passages is the same: Salvation instead of destruction. In my opinion the *mahpekâ* in God's heart can only mean that God suffers for the salvation of Israel. God undergoes the same fate as Sodom. This, in a special way, underscores Rudolph's remark at the end of his discussion of the next verse: 'Hier ist Evangelium im Alten Testament'.

Why is Admah and Zeboim mentioned and not Sodom and Gomorrah? We have the same motif and the same function whether the former pair or the latter is used, and the four are clearly associated in three other passages (Gn 10:19, 14:2.8, Dt 29:22). Why then only here no word about Sodom and Gomorrah? The most obvious answer is that given by Gunkel, Zimmerli and Westermann (1981:229): Hosea knew and used a variant form of the tradition in which Admah and Zeboim had the same function as Sodom and Gomorrah. This would, however, require two other hypotheses. First, the combination of the two pairs in the three passages cited above have to be declared secondary. This may not cause a problem in the late exilic passage of Deuteronomy 29:22, but it does in the Genesis passages. Westermann (1976:699) declares Admah and Zeboim to be an addition in Genesis 10:19 and later (1981:229) he says it is 'probably' so. He is then forced to accept a combination of a northern and a southern tradition in Genesis 14 (which is more or less what Gunkel also does). But where would the 'northern tradition' come from if not from the south? This highlights a second forced hypothesis: Admah and Zeboim cannot be cities thought to have been in the Dead Sea vicinity. It is indeed what Gunkel gives in to when he surmises that these two cities were 'perhaps' ('vielleicht') not originally situated near the Dead Sea. But this is a kind of begging the question into which he is forced. If we are to accept a special northern tradition ('Sondertradition'), it would be natural to expect that tradition to be about northern cities. The Dead Sea region suits the topographical requirements excellently, but such a wasteland is not found in the Northern Kingdom. Moreover, a single passage from a northern prophet remains a precarious basis for a hypothesis already burdened by several questionable assumptions. For these reasons it seems better to accept *one* Sodom and Gomorrah tradition in which Admah and Zeboim (and Zoar) also featured. Various selections could be made from the cities mentioned in the tradition. The tradition could, if we count Zoar as well, be called a tale of one, two, four or five cities in various combinations. In fact we do not only have two – which one would have expected if there were two 'Sondertraditionen' – but five such combinations of place names:

Sodom

Sodom and Gomorrah

Sodom, Gomorrah, Admah and Zeboim

Admah and Zeboim

Sodom, Gomorrah, Admah, Zeboim and Zoar

This argument is also in keeping with what we have found above about the content of the Sodom and Gomorrah tradition, viz that the wickedness of Sodom as seen by the prophets is not fundamentally different from that as seen by the Sodom Cycle. The cycle has the same awareness of the social manifestation of violence as the typical prophetic perspective of the eighth to the sixth century BCE – which is not surprising, since it dates from the same period as the critical prophets (cf above, p 43). The evidence is pointing increasingly towards one basic tradition manifesting in several functions.

Our last reference to Sodom on the Old Testament is **Lamentations 4:6**. It is part of an alphabetic poem in the destruction of Jerusalem and occurs in the *waw* strophe. There are three main sections of which the first (vv 1-16) speaks of Zion in the third person singular, while the second (vv 17-20) opens with the first person plural (Kraus) and the last (vv 21-22) uses the second person singular. Commentators are mostly agreed as to the use of the Sodom motif in this passage. In verses 3-6 the terrible lot of the children serves as a manifestation of the catastrophe which has befallen Jerusalem (Weiser). The interesting thing about the reference to Sodom is the way in which the two main aspects of the Sodom motif, viz the symbol of wickedness and the symbol of destruction, are combined here. In the first stich the iniquity (*'âwon*) of the people is said to be greater than the sin (*ḥaṭṭâ't*) of Sodom (cf Gottwald 1962:16, 69). In the second stich Sodom is qualified by a passive participle *hᵃpûkâ*, 'she who has been overturned', the same root found so often in the Sodom passages of the Old Testament. Therefore both the wickedness of Sodom and her devastation are used in the same reference. This is not coincidence, since the poem argues from punishment to guilt: If the punishment of Jerusalem is greater than that of Sodom, then it follows that her sins must also be greater (Gottwald, Weiser, Kraus, Plöger). From this follows, again, that the words *'âwon* and *ḥaṭṭâ't*, both of which may refer to a sin committed and to the resulting punishment, are used ambiguously in our text (cf Jr 11:10, Ezk 4:5, Lm 2:14; Jr 2:22, Hs 9:7; Is 5:18, Jr 5:25, Lm 4:13; Zch 14:19; cf Gn 18:20 where *ḥaṭṭâ't* is used in the former sense, and Gn 19:15 where *'âwon* is used in the latter sense). The sin of Jerusalem and her punishment are greater than the sin and punishment of Sodom. This can be substantiated as follows: The punishment of Sodom was an over-turning (*hpk*) which lasted only a moment (*règa'*), but the punishment of Jerusalem is the prolonged suffering so cruelly obvious in the slow languishing of the children (vv 4-5, cf Weiser). All of this goes hand-in-hand with an awareness of the social aspect of Israel's sin (v 13), which is a characteristic of the prophetic passages where the Sodom motif is found, and has the further similarity to some of these passages that the leaders are criticised (cf v 13 with Is 1:10 and Jr 23:14). Moreover, the element of hope, albeit very subdued, is not lacking in the lament (v 22), which in turn is comparable to two other prophetic 'Sodom-passages' (Ezk 16, Hs 11:8). Our conclusion is, then, that the eye-witness of Jerusalem's devastation in 587 BCE, the poet of the lament, used the Sodom tradition in fundamentally the same way as the pre-exilic prophets and that this use of the motif does not testify to a different or alternative tradition from the one manifested in Genesis 18-19.

In conclusion it remains to be said that there are in the Old Testament a few possible allusions to the Sodom and Gomorrah tradition where, however, the cities are not actually mentioned.

In Isaiah 34:9-11 the devastation of Edom is described in terms very similar to that of Babylon in Isaiah 13:19-21. The reference to 'the cities which Yahweh overturned' (*hpk*) in Jeremiah 20:16 (surprisingly overlooked in Gunkel's list of 'Anspielungen', 1910:216) is remarkable in that it is used in a curse on the man who had brought the tidings of the prophet's birth to Jeremiah's father. The value of this evident allusion to the cities of the Dead Sea plain is that it shows to what an extent their destruction had already become proverbial or at least so fixed an element in tradition that it could be applied to individual people. Even an oblique reference like the present one is assumed to be readily understandable by the sixth century audience. In Psalm 11:6 Yahweh is said to cause sulphur (*goprît*) and fire (*'eš*) to rain (*mṭr*) on the wicked. These are the words used in Genesis 19:24 to describe the destruction of Sodom and Gomorrah (although the word-order differs there), and the presentation conjures up the idea of utter destruction so typical of the Sodom and Gomorrah tradition. Perhaps this is also contained in the wish uttered in Psalm 140:11 that fiery coals fall on the wicked people (*'âdâm râ'*, v 2) and that they themselves fall into pits (cf Gn 14:10), but only the word *'eš* is common to the psalm and the Sodom tradition (unless, as is sometimes proposed, a textual emendation is made in order to produce the verb *mṭr*).

We can now summarise the motifs associated with the Sodom and Gomorrah tradition in the Hebrew Old Testament outside the Book of Genesis.

1. From the eighth to the sixth centuries the Sodom and Gomorrah motif constantly functions as the symbol of wickedness and as the symbol of total destruction, sometimes in one text (Ezk 16, Lm 4:6).

2. The sin of Sodom and Gomorrah is often seen by the pre-exilic prophets as social in nature (Isaiah, Jeremiah, Ezekiel), or the punishment is associated with such wickedness (Amos); the same perspective can be seen in Lamentations 4.

3. Once (Jr 23:14) it is seen as sexual sin, while the idolatry spoken of by Hosea in association with the Admah and Zeboim motif also has such overtones.

4. Those who are compared to Sodom and Gomorrah or whose destruction is compared to that of the cities of the plain can be Jerusalem/Judah or Ephraim/Israel, but the same can be said of other nations or cities (Babylon in Is 13:19, Jr 50:40; Edom in Jr 49:18; Moab and Ammon in Zph 2:9), and sometimes a specific group of leaders are seen as 'Sodomites' (Is 1:10, Jr 23:14, Lm 4:6.7.13).

5. The social motif is always associated with Judah/Israel, and the motif of a wasteland like Sodom is, with the exception of the late exilic Deuteronomy 29:22, always associated with other nations (be it in the eighth, seventh or sixth century).

6. If the reference to Sodom in Isaiah 3:9 is a gloss, the social function of the Sodom motif has been developed in late exilic times to include favouritism in the administering of justice, which would be a prelude to later Jewish use of the tradition.

71

7. In the Deuteronomistic tradition the motif functions to illustrate the punishment for breach of covenant (Dt 29:22) and to show the innate wickedness of Israel's enemies (Dt 32:32).

8. Twice the Sodom tradition is used to achieve a positive end, viz in Hosea 11, where God himself undergoes the lot of Admah and Zeboim/ Sodom, and in Ezekiel 16 where Sodom and the other cities are restored to happiness by God.

3.3. Conclusions

Let us now take the three summaries of the predominant motifs of the Sodom and Gomorrah traditions and their functions given above (pp 47-48, 55-56, 71-72) and palimpsest them, so to speak, onto each other. My intention is not to be repetitive, but to construct a picture of which traditional motifs with which functions were known in which periods rather than to reconstruct 'the original' Sodom and Gomorrah tradition. We can take due heed of the dampening effect on over-enthusiastic attempts in such a direction provided by Van Seters's scepticism (Van Seters 1975:157; cf above, p 24), but we still have the responsibility to use the data that we do have to explain the phenomenon of the recurrence of the same names and motifs in various environments.

The earliest elements underlying the Sodom and Gomorrah tradition are ancient reminiscences of a catastrophe in the Dead Sea plain.

During the pre-monarchic time the following at least was in circulation about our theme: The city of Sodom was already associated with the Israelite tradition of Abraham. The patriarch's superiority over and dissociation from the king of Sodom already suggests an unfavourable view of the city. The settlement of Abraham's kinsman in Sodom and the motif of the paradise-like vicinity were also known by this time. The emphasis on the well-watered country only makes sense if the opposite character of the vicinity was to be explained in this way. Therefore it suggests that the motif of destruction was also known in this time. A non-Israelite story of several gods who visited the area and a non-Israelite story of the origin of Moab and Ammon also hail from this time. It therefore appears plausible that the basic motifs of what we call the Sodom tradition could have already existed in this period, viz a wicked city which was destroyed and thus became a barren wasteland.

During the period of the monarchy, about the eighth century BCE, Sodom and its neighbour cities were regarded as being excluded from Canaan, thus from the Promised Land. The motif of the erstwhile paradise laid waste, which, together with the motif of exclusion, requires an unfavourable view of Sodom, also occurs in this period. Often the prophets use Sodom c s as symbols of wickedness (social and sexual) and of desolation and this may be in comparison to Judah, Israel or other nations. Amos's use of the fixed formula suggests independence from the story in Genesis 18-19 (apart from considerations about a date later than Amos for the cycle).

The Sodom Cycle itself was composed in the seventh century BCE and thus could not influence the preaching of the earlier prophets. There are also signs that Zephaniah, who comes from roughly the same period, possibly somewhat later, used the Sodom and Gomorrah motifs independently from the cycle. It is therefore legitimate to say that the use of Sodom and Gomorrah c s in the service of the critical moral preaching of the eighth century prophets was independent from the Sodom Cycle in Genesis 18-19.

In the sixth century the typical prophetic perspective was represented by Jeremiah and Ezekiel, while the latter was the only one to announce a restoration for Sodom. There is evidence of literary dependence of Ezekiel 16:50 on the Genesis story.

During various stages of the exilic period the tradition was maintained. The story of Genesis 18-19 was known and was provided with an extension (Gn 19:29). The prophetic perspective lived on (Lm 4) and in the later phases of this period the tradition was used to ridicule foreign kings and to criticise favouritism in the administering of justice.

All of this does not mean that the tradition used by the pre-exilic prophets is *older* than the tradition used by the author of Genesis 18-19. It is the same tradition with the same motifs and the same basic function. The literary genres differ and the nuances and emphases differ, but there is no fundamental difference in the view taken of Sodom and Gomorrah, of what their inhabitants did and of what happened to them. This goes not only for the basic motifs of wickedness and destruction, but also for the social aspect (of oppressive violence and injustice to the powerless strangers) and for the concern shared by Genesis 18:17-33, Hosea and Ezekiel for the saving justice/mercy of God. We will therefore have to reject the sharp distinction between the Genesis story and the prophets made by Von Rad (1964:185) and others.

Our study suggests that there was in existence, already before the monarchy, a complex of motifs which could be called 'the Sodom tradition'. It was this tradition from which the author of the Sodom Cycle drew the material for his story, and it was the same tradition from which the prophets drew the Sodom motifs used by them. In view of this fact, and in view of the widespread use of the tradition, it is impossible to tie it to a specific circle of tradition, institution, school or period. Both the common source of the independent usages of the theme and the fact that some texts *were* dependent on the Sodom Cycle entitle us to speak of 'the Sodom tradition' in the singular. We are, however, equally justified in using the plural 'Sodom traditions', for the motifs were used in different times and different places with different emphases and in different genres. In the former case we would merely be referring to the forest, and in the latter to the various trees.

4. Sodom and Gomorrah in early Jewish literature

When we turn to the use and meaning of the Sodom and Gomorrah traditions in the early Jewish literature, we are confronted with various difficult problems. They pertain to the vastness of the field so designated. First, we have the problem of definition. What is 'early Jewish literature'? It could be argued that most of the New Testament and some other early Christian writings also form part of what is called 'early Jewish'. For the sake of convenience we will, however, keep the two separate and exclude all Christian writings from the Jewish literature relevant to us. We will take 'Jewish literature' to mean literature from various currents within Judaism in the time between the Old Testament and the Talmud. This touches on our second problem: The historical limits to what could be called 'early' Jewish literature are relative and lines drawn to divide periods are often arbitrary. Nevertheless we are bound to draw them in order to maintain a grip on the material. In our case the often recognised caesura of the completion of the Talmud, into which much of the Sodom and Gomorrah tradition has found its way, will be applied. Although the Babylonian Talmud was only completed in the fifth century, the Talmud contains material from roughly the same period as the corpus of Christian literature prior to the major hiatus of 313 CE, when Christianity became the official religion of the Roman Empire. So the Rabbinic and the Christian uses of the Sodom and Gomorrah traditions will be comparable, coming as they do from the first three to four centuries CE.

Our terms of reference, then, require us to study the use of the Sodom and Gomorrah traditions in the Apocrypha, the Pseudepigrapha, the works of Flavius Josephus, of Philo, and the vast field of Rabbinic literature. Naturally we should also take cognizance of the Qumran literature and the popular material of the Targum tradition.

The terms 'Apocrypha' and 'Pseudepigrapha' are not always used with clear distinction in meaning. Literature called 'Pseudepigrapha' by some scholars (e g Herford 1933, Eissfeldt 1965, Weiser 1966, Denis 1968, Rost 1971) are sometimes called 'Apocrypha' by others (e g Bonsirven 1953). The first group of authors also differ among themselves (e g Eissfeldt and Weiser who regard 3 Maccabees as one of the Apocrypha, while Rost and Riessler regard it as a pseudepigraphon). 'Pseudepigrapha' is, further, a misnomer, since some books within the Hebrew canon (e g Daniel) and within the Greek Old Testament (e g Baruch) also have pseudepigraphic names, while some 'Pseudepigrapha' (e g Jubilees) do not have a 'false name' (cf Eissfeldt 1965:573). We shall use the term 'Apocrypha' to refer to the Jewish writings from the last three centuries BCE that were included in the Greek canon but not in the Hebrew canon, and the term 'Pseudepigrapha' to refer to the Jewish writings from the same period that were not included in these canons but were held in esteem by certain communities only (cf Eissfeldt 1965:573, Rost 1971:22-24).

4.1. The Apocrypha

In the Apocryphal books of the Septuagint the Sodomites (*Sodomitai*, 3 Mac 2:5) are mentioned once, but the names of Sodom and Gomorrah do not occur. There are, however, several clear references to the tradition of the destruction of these cities.

The earliest instance is **Ben Sira 16:7-10**. Here the only explicit reference to Lot in the Apocrypha is found. It is said that Lot's place of sojourn (*paroikia*) was not spared. Lot's place of sojourn is Sodom where he lived as a *ger*. In our text both aspects of the Sodom symbolism are found. On the one hand the destruction of Sodom is mentioned (*ouk exilasato, ouk èleèsen, exèrmenous*) and on the other the wickedness of its inhabitants is mentioned as the reason for the destruction (*hous ebdeluxato dia tèn hyperèphanian autón, en hamartiais autón*). Their wickedness in general is coupled to the idea of hubris which is their special sin. This tallies with the context in which another example is given of the destruction which befalls the arrogant. In verse 7 it is said that the giants of ancient times who revolted 'in their strength' (*tè ischui autón*) were not pardoned. Obviously it is God who did not pardon them and therefore it is he against whom they revolted. The giants of ancient times refer to the giants of Genesis 6:4 (cf Ginzberg 1900:75-76). They are associated with the 'Watchers' (the fallen angels) and the generation of the flood. These groups are often connected to the people of Sodom (3 Mac 2:4, Jub 20:5-6, Lk 17:26-29, 2 Pt 2:4-8, Jude 6-7, and several times in the Samaritan Memar Marqah; cf Lührmann 1972:130-132, Hollander & De Jonge 1985:307-308 and discussion below, pp 80, 84, 120-124). The 'six hundred thousand warriors' in verse 10 refers to Israel who left Egypt. According to Exodus 12:37 this was the number of men, excluding the women and children, who started the desert journey (cf Lamparter 1972a:76) and who perished because of their sins before entering the Promised Land (cf Nu 14:22-23). The motif of the Sodomites is therefore accompanied by two other examples of God's punishment for sin, viz the ancient giants and Israel's wilderness generation. Although there is no explicit reference to the place of Lot's sojourn, two verses in the section of which our text forms part (vv 1-14) also seem to allude to the Sodom tradition. In verse 4 it is said that a tribe (*phyle*) of lawless people becomes deserted. It is possible that the verb *erèmóthèsetai* can mean 'to make desert (*erèmos*)' in addition to 'lay waste'. The former may be intended here, as suggested by the New English Bible. Then *phyle* may mean 'tribal land', but in the light of Genesis 19:25 it seems possible for people as well as the land to be thought of as having been made a desert (cf Hebrew *hpk* and Greek *erèmoein*; Hebrew *'ârîm, kikkâr* and Greek *polis*; Hebrew *yoš*bê hè'ârîm* and Greek *phyle*). In any case the devastation motif goes well with the Sodom motif a few verses further on. The same goes for the second allusion. In verse 6 we hear that fire breaks out among sinners and that a rebellious nation is burnt up (*ekkaiein*) by wrath. This fits in very well with the fire (*'eš*) by which Sodom was destroyed according to Genesis 19:24.

On these grounds we may conclude that Ben Sira used the Sodom motif in literary dependence on the Genesis story, but that he was also influenced by other lines of tradition as we can see from the association of Sodom with the ancient giants and the motif of six hundred thousand warriors. Ben Sira represents the current of traditional Jewish piety in which the Scriptures and temple cult were emphasised over against what would become central to Pharisaic Judaism, like angels, demons and life after death (Brockington 1961:76). This religious background goes hand in hand with the Israelite sapiential tradition, but is not as deeply influenced by Hellenistic philosophy as the other apocryphal wisdom book, the Wisdom of Solomon. Therefore we may say that the typical Sodom motifs of wickedness and destruction were also used by the higher circles of cultically-minded Judaism of the early second century BCE, to which Ben Sira belonged. The tendency of our passage is to warn that God's wrath and punishment is as real as his mercy and forgiveness (cf vv 11-12). It is in keeping with the general orientation of Ben Sira's concept of God, where awesomeness and mercy stand side by side (cf Brockington 1961:82-83). This religious background, which some have wrongly called 'Sadducaean' (cf Herford 1933:204-205), makes the use of the Sodom and Gomorrah tradition a natural thing. We may even wonder why it is used so obliquely when it lends itself so well to Ben Sira's purpose.

The second apocryphal passage is, like Ben Sira, part of the sapiential tradition of Israel: the **Wisdom of Solomon 10:6-9**. This passage is part of the opening section of the third division of the book (Sap 10-19), which is characterised by the theme of God's intervention in history to the benefit of his people and the detriment of the wicked (cf Rost 1971:42). Exactly this is what we find in our passage. Wisdom, which coincides with piety, is extolled for being the principle which made success possible in the past (for such a historical review in the service of sapiential concern, cf Sir 44-50); failure and calamities result from the opposite, folly, which coincides with wickedness. Examples of both wisdom and folly are given. Adam, Noah, Abraham, Lot, Jacob, Joseph, Moses, Israel in Egypt and in the desert all serve as examples of the benefits of wisdom (Sap 10:1 - 11:14). On the other hand Cain and the cities of the Pentapolis serve as examples of the catastrophes caused by folly (a similar list of illustrations of folly, which includes the Sodomites, is found in Memar Marqah 6:2). It is interesting that Cain, who murdered his brother (Gn 4:8), is thought of as the one who caused the deluge (vv 3-4). This may be explained by the fact that the first deed of violence, that of Cain (Gn 4:1-16), naturally leads via the genealogies of Genesis 4:17-26 and 5:1-32 to the story of the giants of old (often associated with the Sodomites, cf Sir 16:7-8, 3 Mac 2:4) and the story of the flood which came over the world because of the proliferation of violence (cf Gn 6:11). If this is correct, the next example makes good sense: The second event in the history of humankind in which, according to the ancient traditions of Israel, violence was punished by a catastrophe, was the destruction of the cities of the Dead Sea plain. Therefore the two illustrations of folly suit each other quite well (cf Gunkel 1910:77, 214):

violence (Gn 4:8)	violence (Gn 19:5.9)
all involved (Gn 6:5.11.12)	all involved (Gn 19:4)
destruction by water (Gn 6:17)	destruction by fire (Gn 19:24)
one man and family saved (Gn 6:18)	one man and family saved (Gn 19:15)

Lot is not mentioned by name in our text, but it is a characteristic of the whole passage (cf also Sap 19) that the traditionally familiar figures are referred to by means of unmistakable features of their respective characters. He is, however, called a 'good men' (*dikaios*, like six of the seven 'good men' in the list of wisdom's achievements, cf Winston 1982:211) and is therefore considered quite differently from Jubilees 16:8-9 where Lot is severely judged as the arch-example of incest (cf below, pp 83-84). On the other hand his wife became a pillar of salt because of her unbelief (she was an *apistousè psychè*, v 7), which shows that unbelief/impiety is the opposite of wisdom and therefore equals folly. The motif of the barren wasteland is also present here (for the useless fruit, cf Dt 32:32 and pp 57-58 above). The author follows the narratives of the Book of Genesis faithfully, and therefore we are entitled to look upon his term *Pentapolis* as an oversight. He speaks of the *five* cities that were destroyed and can therefore only mean the five occurring together in Genesis 14. But one of these five, Zoar, was spared on account of Lot so that it would have been more correct to speak of *four* cities that were destroyed.

In the concluding passage of the third division of the book Sodom appears as indirectly as in the opening passage. In the Wisdom of Solomon 19:13-17 the Egyptians are said to have suffered justly for their own wickedness (v 13, *ponèria*). Then they are compared to the men of Sodom. While the Sodomites refused strangers like Lot kindness (v 14a, cf Gn 19:9), the Egyptians enslaved people who were their benefactors (v 14b, cf Gn 41:39-40.55-57). They were worse than the Sodomites in that they first freely accepted the guests and shared their rights with them (v 16, cf Gn 45:19-20, 47:6.12), only to turn around and oppress them. This is a somewhat contrived comparison (cf Lamparter) since Genesis 19 can also be interpreted to the effect that the Sodomites first accepted Lot as a guest (*gwr*, Gn 19:9) and then turned against him. In verse 17 the blindness with which the Sodomites were struck (Gn 19:11) is related to the 'blindness' of the Egyptians (Ex 10:21-23; the same word, *aorasia*, is used in Sap 19:17 and in Gn 19:11 LXX). The last half of verse 17 is ambiguous and can be taken to refer to the Sodomites groping for their doors (which would deviate from the Genesis text where they grope for Lot's door) or to the Egyptians groping for theirs. In any case the point of the passage is that there is an *episkopè* waiting for the Sodomites (v 15) and, *a fortiori*, this must mean an even worse judgement in store for the Egyptians. Volz (1934:246) takes the *episkopè* referred to here as a second judgement which leads to punishment in hell. This is probable, since the judgement of the ancient Sodomites (and Egyptians) is seen as something yet to come and can only take place after the resurrection. In conclusion we may compare the relative preference of the Sodomites to others with the same use of the motif in Ezekiel 16:48 and especially Matthew 10:15, 11:24, Lk 10:12; (cf above, p 66 and below, pp 118-120).

Our texts are part of a first century BCE wisdom book and as such are excellent examples of a sapiential interpretation of the Sodom and Gomorrah tradition. The basic motifs of wickedness and punishment are again present, but are put to use in the service of Jewish wisdom which had undergone Hellenistic influence. As we can see in especially the book's concept of the soul and of life after death, we have here the religious background of a first century Jew who had been in contact with Hellenistic philosophy of a Philonic type (Volz 1934:59; cf Eissfeldt 1965:601 on the stylistic features, Weiser 1966:359 on the philosophical aspects, and Rost 1971:43-44 on the combination of Hellenistic and biblical wisdom).

Our last apocryphal passage is **3 Maccabees 2:5.** It is part of the prayer of the high priest Simon in response to the endeavour of (Ptolemy IV) Philopator to enter the sanctuary of the temple in Jerusalem. Philopator, fresh from victory, is expressly said to have acted overbearingly and rashly (*hybrei kai thrasei*, v 21), and is punished by being humiliated by God. In the prayer, which leads up to the divine miracle, several examples are mentioned of God's punishment of overbearing wickedness: The giants of old (v 4; cf Ben Sira 16:7, where the giants are also mentioned with reference to their overbearing acts), the Sodomites (v 5), and the pharaoh who pursued Israel on their way out of Egypt (vv 6-7a; cf Ex 14; also Memar Marqah 4:5.12, 6:2) are examples of what happens to people who act overbearingly against God. The Sodomites practiced *hyperèphania* and were distinguished (*diadèlous*) for their wicked deeds (*kakiais*), for which God punished them with fire and brimstone. Here both aspects of the Sodom motif stand side by side and wickedness and punishment are equally emphasised. However, as the hubris motif is used in addition to the generic term *kakia*, the focal point of the wickedness is represented as insolence (cf Is 13:19, Ezk 16:49-50, Ze 2:9-10, Sir 16:8-10, TLevi 14:7). Contrary to Ben Sira, who also combines the traditional motifs of Sodom and the exodus as well as the hubris motif, our text from the first century BCE exemplifies a strong anti-foreigner attitude and uses the Sodom tradition for this purpose.

4.2. The Pseudepigrapha

Sodom and Gomorrah occur frequently in the Pseudepigrapha. Our first set of texts come from the Testaments of the Twelve Patriarchs where the tradition is found no less than five times. If we accept an earlier date for the Testament of Levi and the Testament of Naphtali than for the remaining testaments (cf Rost 1971:109), three of these occurrences belong to the oldest parts of the Testaments, i e around 150 BCE (cf Denis 1970:58). We shall look at them one by one (in spite of the misgivings of De Jonge, 1979:192, about the study of individual passages in the Testaments I do not see another way of examining the evidence of a limited theme in the Testaments).

One of the clearest instances of the use of the tradition is found in the **Testament of Levi 14:6.** This verse is part of a passage (TLevi 14:1 - 15:4) which is structured as follows: Introduction (TLevi 14:1), future sins (TLevi 14:2-8), punishment (TLevi 15:1-4; cf Hollander & De Jonge 1985:169, from whose analysis my own deviates slightly). In verse 6 itself the Sodom and Gomorrah tradition is explicity used to underline sexual sins. Israel's sexual relations (*meixis*) will 'be like Sodom and Gomorrah'. This is elaborately expounded in the verse as 'polluting married women', 'deflowering virgins of Jerusalem', having intercourse with 'whores and adulterous women' and taking 'heathen girls'. Whereas the last of these sins is about unclean marriage, the others are straightforward sexual aberrations (whores are also mentioned in v 5). The comparison to Sodom and Gomorrah obviously draws on Genesis 19:5. No distinction is made between the homosexual aspect of the biblical passage and the sexual libertinism criticised in our passage. Sodom and Gomorrah function as the arch-examples of sexual sinners. However, in the context a number of other motifs are encountered which we have often found to be associated with Sodom and Gomorrah. Wickedness in general is mentioned in the opening verse, self-enrichment precedes the list of sexual sins in verse 6, hubris as a sinful attitude is mentioned three times in verse 7, and the idea of a wasteland is applied to the temple in the first verse of the section on punishment (TLevi 15:1; cf Hollander & De Jonge 1985:170 for references to *erèmos* in connection with the temple). The whole passage, concerned as it is with social misdemeanour, smacks of the prophetic use of the Sodom and Gomorrah tradition. I do not argue that the use of the sexual, social, hubris, punishment and wasteland motifs have been suggested to our author by the prophetic use of these motifs. The emphasis on the sexual aspect with specific reference to Sodom and Gomorrah is too strong to associate these other motifs as closely with the two cities. Our text does suggest, however, that the Sodom and Gomorrah tradition functioned, with variations in emphasis, in fairly constant environments - always relating in some way to the basic symbolism of wickedness and punishment.

In the **Testament of Naphtali 3:4** we find an even more specialised use of the Sodom tradition (here, as elsewhere in the Testaments, with the exception of TLevi 14:6, Sodom is mentioned without Gomorrah). The whole chapter is concerned with 'the order of nature' (*taxis physeós*; cf Koester 1968:531, Berger 1970:37), which is also found in the thought of Philo (Aet Mund 31,34; cf Abr 135; see below, p 88). Having warned against the danger of self-enrichment (*pleonexia*, the same word found in TLevi 14:6) in verse 1, the rest of the passage is an exhortation to recognise in creation the *kyrios* who made it all, and therefore to avoid changing the order that he has put into nature. One positive example and three negative examples are given to stress the point. The positive example is the sun, moon and stars who do not change their order and are therefore worthy of being imitated in this respect (v 2). The negative examples are the gentiles who have changed the order of nature in following idols instead of the

Creator of nature (v 3), the Sodomites (v 4) and the Watchers (v 5). The latter are the fallen angels associated with Genesis 6:4 (cf above, pp 76-77 on Ben Sira 16:8-10), and therefore the reference is clearly to their unnatural sexual union with human girls (cf the motif of devastation and a wasteland associated with the Watchers in v 5). In this context the changing of its order by Sodom can only refer to the homosexual aspirations of the Sodomites mentioned in Genesis 19:5.

The next passage starts two verses further in the **Testament of Naphtali 4:1** and is closely related to the previous one by referring back to it in the very first words (*tauta legó*). Here mention is made of the general wickedness of the heathens and the Sodomites (respectively *ponèria* and *anomia*). So Sodom is again used as symbol of wickedness. But the following verses are about the punishment that is to follow sin, and, although it is not explicitly linked to Sodom, the symbol of wickedness is again found in the company of the punishment motif.

As Hollander and De Jonge (1985:359) remark, the **Testament of Asher 7:1** 'connects the following prediction of the collective future of the sons of Asher (Israel) with the preceding description of the destiny of individual persons through the example of Sodom.' The city 'remained ignorant' (*ègnoèse*) of the angels of the Lord who, according to Genesis 19:1, were sent to Sodom. The verb *agnoein* has no sexual connotations and therefore the translation 'das an des Herren Engeln sich versündigte' (Riessler 1928:1230) is not successful. The passage implies that the Sodomites sinned as a result of not recognising the angels. Here the emphasis is not on their sin, but on their punishment. The punishment is severe: The Sodomites ('Sodom' is used in the figure of synecdochy) perished forever. This is the exact opposite of what Ezekiel expected (Ezk 16:53.55; cf above, p 63).

Our last text from the Testaments is the **Testament of Benjamin 9:1**, again the opening verse of a chapter (cf TNaph 4:1, TAsh 7:1). Here the sexual function of the Sodom motif is again quite obvious: *porneusete gar porneian Sodomón* ('You will go awhoring with the whoring of Sodom') and *en gynaixi strènous* ('wanton deeds with women'). In the same verse the punishment of destruction is mentioned, but this time adapted to the needs of the author. All will not perish like the Sodomites did; a few will survive. Could we see in this a suggestion of the saving of Lot, his family, and the town of Zoar (Gn 19:21)?

Sodom is also mentioned in another text, the **Testament of Abraham**

82

6:13 (β-Recension from the third century CE, based on an original in Hebrew of some two centuries earlier, cf Denis 1970:36). However, this reference does not focus on Sodom, but on Abraham. The story is told of two visits to Abraham by the Archangel Michael, of a dream by Isaac, Abraham's ascension to heaven, return to earth and death. The story makes more use of Genesis 18 than of Genesis 19. It extols the virtue of hospitality (which, according to Riessler 1928:1332-1333, speaks for an origin in Essene circles; cf, however, Denis 1970:35). As such its dependence on Genesis 18:1-16 is quite understandable. In our passage Abraham says that, as he was washing the feet of his guest, he recognised them as being the same feet he had once washed at Mamre (cf Gn 18:4, where it is not said that Abraham himself washed the feet of the guests), and when he asked about the way the guest was going, he was told that Michael was on his way to save Lot from Sodom. The importance of the reference is that it shows that in the first century BCE the Sodom Cycle of Genesis 18-19 could be used for other purposes than the conventional wickedness/punishment symbolism. In this case the idea of hospitality is appropriately developed along the lines of Genesis 18 (cf Heb 13:2).

From Hasmonean times, probably between 161 and 152 BCE (VanderKam 1977:283-285), come the references to Sodom and Gomorrah in Jubilees 16, 20, 22 and 36 (cf Rost 1971:100). This originally Hebrew book (cf Charles 1895:ix) bears evidence of an anti-Hellenistic attitude informed by apocalyptic sentiments (cf the supernatural revelation of mysteries, the disclosures made by an angel; Herford 1933:225, 229) and Essene sympathies (VanderKam 1977:258-283; cf Denis 1970:161). As a 'Little Genesis' it is dependent on the Book of Genesis, which it intends to supplement.

In the first of the relevant texts, **Jubilees 16:5-9**, the 'Angel of the Countenance' is telling about their (first person plural) visit to Abraham at Mamre and their announcement that a son is to be born to Abraham (cf Gn 18:1-16). In verse 5 the destruction of Sodom and Gomorrah by fire and sulphur is mentioned with substantiating reference to the sins of the inhabitants, viz general wickedness, injustice and sexual impurity. Verse 6 gives the purpose of the destruction of the two cities, that is, we are shown the function of the tradition: It is a warning that God will do likewise to places where the impurity of Sodom (this time Gomorrah is not added) is committed (cf Jub 20:5-6; Philo, Abr 136.137, says that the destruction took place so that the rest of the world would not be contaminated). Verses 7-9 roughly continue the story of Genesis 19. Lot was saved 'because God remembered Abraham'. He and his daughters were therefore not saved on account of their own merits, but because of Abraham (cf

Gn 19:29; also Gn 19:1-3, and the Wisdom of Solomon 10:6, where Lot is a 'good man' endowed with wisdom and saved for that reason). This is not surprising, since the following verses (vv 8-9) severely criticise the union of Lot with his daughters as incest which had been unheard of before that time. For this deed their offspring will be punished in a way comparable to the punishment of Sodom (v 9). It is unlikely that this should be taken to mean that the Moabites and the Ammonites would be destroyed by fire and sulphur, since there is no evidence for such a tradition. It is, however, clearly intended to mean that there will be no member of these peoples left when the Day of Judgement arrives. Reference is not made to the way in which they will be destroyed, but to the completeness of the destruction. Sexual sin and extermination as punishment are again present in the use of the Sodom and Gomorrah tradition, and the theme functions as a warning.

In the second passage, **Jubilees 20:5-6,** we find basically the same. Here Abraham addresses his sons and grandsons (v 1) with various injunctions, viz to love their neighbours and to practice justice (v 2), to keep the commandment of circumcision and to avoid sexual transgressions (vv 3-4). Marriage to heathen girls is mentioned on a par with sexual immorality, which we have also seen in the Testaments (cf *thygateras ethnón*, TLevi 15:6, here called 'the daughters of Canaan'). As in Ben Sira 16:7 and 3 Maccabees 2:4, the giants of ancient times occur together with the Sodomites, here in a sexual context (cf Hollander & De Jonge 1985:307). The fact that Gomorrah is not mentioned in verse 5 but that it does occur in the parallelism of verse 6, points to the probability that the giants and Sodom occur in a fixed combination. In verse 6 we have a parallelistic use of Sodom and Gomorrah, where the curse of Sodom is used in a warning (cf Jub 16:6) to the sons and grandsons listening to Abraham and the curse of Gomorrah in a warning to the offspring of these people (cf the parallelistic use of the two cities in Is 1:10, Zeph 2:9).

In **Jubilees 22:22** the punishment of total extermination is illustrated with reference to the annihilation of the Sodomites. Those who can expect such punishment are they who practise idolatry. **Jubilees 36:10** contains the clearest possible use of the Sodom tradition in the service of eschatological damnation. Isaac warns his sons that anyone among them who plans evil against his brother will be destroyed with his offspring (v 9). The details of a following and final judgement, which must therefore take place at the end of time (cf Volz 1934:29), are made abundantly clear in the following verse: On the day of God's wrath such a person will find all his property consumed by fire as God had once consumed Sodom (Gomorrah is not mentioned), his name will not be entered into the Book of Life, he will receive everlasting damnation in which all kinds of inflictions will continually be made new. Here the punishment motif has been taken to its logical conclusion. Volz (1934:318) compares this verse with Baruch 4:35 as examples of God's availing himself of fire as an instrument of punishment. That is, of course, quite correct, but it is not so certain that Volz is right in claiming that the Baruch passage also affords an example of the Sodom tradition. Two motifs in Baruch 4:35 are typical of this tradition, viz the fire from God and the resulting wasteland (demons were thought to haunt the desert; cf Mt 12:43, Dancy 1972:45, 195), but the reference to Sodom, if at all present, is very indirect. We should rather compare Jubilees 36:10 to the passages in the New Testament where the Sodom and Gomorrah tradition is used for elaborating on the eschatological Day of Judgement (cf Mt 10:15, 11:23.24, Lk 10:12, 17:28-30, 2 Pt 2:4-8, Jude 6-7; also Sap 19:14-17).

In the **Slavonic Book of Henoch 10:4-6** (first century BCE) we find a catalogue of the types of people for whom the terrible place of hell has been prepared. They include people who commit sorcery (v 4), violence, and social oppression (v 5). According to another version of the text homosexuals of the 'Sodomite' type are also included (cf Strack & Billerbeck [1922-1926] 1965:786 [vol 3]). These types fit what we have already found to be associated with the wickedness of Sodom.

The last of the pseudepigraphical texts to which we shall pay attention are the two references to Sodom and Gomorrah in the **Apocalypse of Ezra 2:19** and **7:12**. In the first verse there is a problem with the text. It is part of a dialogue between God and Ezra. God says: 'I throw fire over Sodom and Gomorrah' (v 19), whereupon the prophet answers: 'Lord, you do justice to us' (v 20). The problem is: Why is the first person plural (*hèmas*) used in a reaction to the announcement of the fire over Sodom and Gomorrah? Riessler (1928:1273) surmises that a part of the text could have fallen out and that we should supply something to the effect of 'I throw fire over you, as once over Sodom and Gomorrah'. This would make the text read smoothly, but it is not necessary. Sodom and Gomorrah may be used symbolically to address the Jews of Ezra's time and therefore be intended for the first century BCE audience of the apocalypse. Such a use of the reference to the two cities would be quite compatible with the similar use in Isaiah 1:10. Why Sodom and Gomorrah (or the new 'Sodom' and 'Gomorrah') are destroyed by fire, is not stated. It is only implied that they are punished for their sins and that this is their justly deserved lot (cf *axios* in v 20).

In the last text (ApEzr 7:12) it is said that anyone who does not believe the book, will be burnt like Sodom and Gomorrah. Again no traditional motifs are provided, but the verse is important in that it provides another example of how the motif of the destruction of Sodom and Gomorrah can be applied to individual people. We have already seen that this happens in the Book of Jeremiah (Jr 20:16, cf above, p 70), where, however, the cities are not mentioned by name. Such a use of the tradition is only possible where it has fossilised in a fixed expression by which total destruction is meant. The Apocalypse of Ezra is to be dated in the first century BCE and to be associated with the Essene current of thought, as can be seen in the typical Essene doctrine of predestination (ApEzr 2:17). Although I do not believe that there is any connexion, it still is interesting to compare the dialogue between a human and God as well as the agonising over his justice with Genesis 18:17-33. The same trait points in the direction of literary dependence on or affinity with 4 Esdras (cf Wahl 1977:3).

4.3. Philo of Alexandria

The massive extent of the works of Philo Alexandrinus, or, as he is also called, Philo Judaeus, has a paradoxical consequence for our study. On the one hand it makes Philo important for our investigation of the *Wirkungs-geschichte* of the Sodom and Gomorrah traditions. On the other hand it compels us to abridge our discussion of Philo's use of it. Fortunately, it is possible to do so because much of what he says about the traditions is reducible to some basic tenets and can therefore be described accordingly. It should also be remembered that the Sodom and Gomorrah traditions feature in Philo's works because they are part of the Torah and not because he is interested in them for their own sake.

Philo (c 25 BCE - c 40 CE; cf Thyen 1965:2301, Schürer 1909e:323) is of great importance because he was probably the most significant exponent of the endeavour to unite Jewish faith and Hellenistic culture (cf Schürer 1909e:322). The religious and philosophical background against which we are to interpret his use of the Sodom and Gomorrah traditions is epitomi-sed by the way Philo presented Plato as a disciple of Moses (cf Colpe 1961:343). Greek philosophy, as represented by Plato, and Jewish reli-gion, as represented by Moses, are combined. But the *primus inter pares* among the two is Jewish religion (cf Heinemann [1929-1932] 1962:557). This is obvious in Philo's apologetic purpose: There is *one* truth and this coincides with the Jewish religion (Colpe 1961:345). Moses and Plato, Judaism and Hellenism, religion and philosophy, revelation and reason – these are ways in which we can describe the polarity in the thought of Philo. Historically, he was the first to introduce the relationship between faith and reason into theology (Colpe 1961:345).

86

These two poles, 'inextricably mixed' as they are (Goodenough 1962:90), are constantly seen in his use of the Sodom and Gomorrah traditions. This is even more obvious in his method of handling the Scriptures. We shall often see how allegory is applied as a technique by which the documents of the Jewish faith are adapted to the demands of Greek philosophy (cf Thyen 1965:2302), especially the ethical demands of Platonism and the stern moral imperative of the Stoa (cf Heinemann [1929-1932] 1962:557).

As in the case of Josephus, Philo's writings contain two extended texts in which he deals with Sodom and Gomorrah, as well as a number of shorter references. In Philo's case we have to work with no less than eleven different writings and therefore we shall begin with the longer passages. First comes *De Abrahamo* 107-118 on Genesis 18 and its allegorical counterpart (Abr 119-132), followed by *De Abrahamo* 133-146 on Genesis 19 and its allegorical exposition (Abr 147-166), after which Philo reverts to Genesis 13 (Abr 204-216) and its allegory (Abr 217-224), and Genesis 14 (Abr 225-235, 236-244). The second extended passage is *Quaestiones in Genesin* Book 4, which deals with Genesis 18-19 almost verse by verse. Having discussed these texts, we shall turn to the shorter and more incidental (but not unimportant) references to the Sodom and Gomorrah traditions.

De Abrahamo 107-118, 119-132 starts by extolling Abraham's kindness. Seeing three travellers approaching, he invites them to enjoy his hospitality without knowing who they are – which, of course, shows his disinterestedness. He is filled with joy to be able to provide for the strangers (Abr 108). They feast (*hestiasthai*) on the goodwill of the host (Abr 110). This prepares the explicit declaration at the end of the passage (Abr 118) that the angelic guests only pretended to eat (a so-called docetic interpretation; cf also QuaestGn 4:9, where it is said that the visitors ate *symbolikós*). Having received the promise of a child from the highest of the three, Sarah recognised something different in their visitors (Abr 113). It is clear that Philo intends to stress the supernatural character of the visitors, and the impact of this will become apparent in the allegorical exposition.

Philo exploits the number three of the visitors and relates it to God. The three visitors are angelic beings, and allegorically stand for the Father of the Universe (*patèr tón holón*) or He who Is (*ho ón*) in the centre, flanked by the Creative Potency (*hè poiètikè*) called 'God' (cf Colson [1935] 1966:63 on the popular etymology of *theos* from *tithèmi*), and the Royal Potency (*hè basilikè*), called 'Lord' (Abr 121). Sometimes, when the mind is pure, it apprehends the central Being with its two potencies as one, and sometimes, when a human can approach Him that Is only through his deeds, it is apprehended as three (Abr 122). This triad, in turn, corresponds to three different types of human temperament (Abr 124). The triple vision (*hè trittè phantasia*) is in fact only one reality – which can be seen in the literal text, i e of Genesis 18:1-16, where the oscillation of singular and plural is taken as proof of this point (Abr 131-132). So Philo uses an important aspect of the Sodom Cycle to further his own concept of God.

In **De Abrahamo 133-146** the text continues with the 'literal' meaning of Genesis 19. The land of the Sodomites is regarded as part of Canaan (cf, however, above, pp 49-51 on Gn 10:19). The wickedness of the Sodomites consists of gluttony, obscenity, and all kinds of pleasures (*plèthè tón allón hèdonón*) (Abr 133). The motifs of their paradise-like land and prolific crops are associated with their sinfulness (Abr 134) and Philo ascribes their iniquity to their wealth (he uses a quotation from Menander for the purpose, cf Colson [1935] 1966:71). The same idea is found in the thought of Josephus (cf below, p 100). Over-indulgence in alcohol and fine foods, the signs of affluent society, are linked to sexual misdemeanour. Not only the violation of the marriages of their fellows, but also homosexuality became the order of the day. Philo regarded sex as appropriate only for begetting children and not for lust (Heinemann [1929-1932] 1962:261-263). Therefore it is understandable that he would regard sterility as a proper condition to result from this kind of aberration (Abr 135). In fact, they were beginning to corrupt the whole human race (Abr 136). Therefore God punished them out of love for the whole of humankind (Abr 137). There follows a detailed description of the destruction. Fire rained from the clouds and the crops were destroyed (Abr 138), buildings and property in the cities (plural, which means that Philo also regarded the whole region as 'Sodom') were reduced to ashes (Abr 139). Special attention is paid to the destruction of the agricultural potential of the land which extends into the crust of the earth as a result of the thunder (*keraunion*) which brought about the catastrophe (Abr 140). Like Josephus, Philo also adduces 'empirical proof' for the correctness of this story: Anyone can go and see for himself that smoke still ascends from the ground, and he will also find one prosperous city which was spared and which fits the description of the prosperity of the ancient wicked cities (Abr 141). In the concluding section of this passage (Abr 142-146) Philo argues that one can infer from the fact that three visitors came to Abraham while only two went to Sodom, that one was the Existent One for whom it was improper to go to the wicked cities, even for the purpose of punishing them.

The allegorical significance of the Sodom story proper follows directly

(**Abr 147-166**). Only the slightest of references to sexuality is made (in Abr 149). The cities of the Sodom vicinity number five (*hè pentapolis*), and these stand for the five human senses (Abr 148). All of them give pleasure, but taste, smell and touch are the most animal-like and relate to gluttony and sex. The remaining two senses relate to philosophy, but hearing is the more feminine in that it is worked upon, while sight is more masculine in that it reaches out actively (Abr 150). This is also a sexual reference (cf Abr 135, where Philo refers to the sexual roles of men and women as active and passive and relates them to the unnatural sex practices of the Sodomites). Philo continues his argument about the value of sight and light (Abr 156-159; cf Klein 1962:69-79) and about the relationship between sight and understanding (Abr 162-163). As philosophy is only possible because of sight, sight was spared when God destroyed the other senses (Abr 164). Accordingly, the fact that Zoar was spared among the five Pentapolis cities means that this city stands for the sense of sight, while the others stand for 'bodily passions' (*hoi sarkos patheis*). It is not said which of the other cities correspond to which of the passions, neither is the partial preference of hearing above the remaining three senses upheld, and it is also not said what the destruction of four of the senses entails. Sight is the smallest that we have, and at the same time the greatest in that it reaches out to the whole world and heaven (Abr 166; cf the statement in Gn 19:20 about Zoar's smallness and the following question in which the negative formulation *ou mikra esti* is used; Colson [1935] 1966:84). There is a close relationship between sight and the soul (Abr 153, where the eyes reflect the condition of the soul and sight is an image of the soul, *eikón psychès*; cf Klein 1962:50-51). Therefore we may interpret Philo's use of the Sodom and Gomorrah tradition as an allegory of the destruction of the body and the continued existence of the soul: One part of the human Pentapolis is spared while the other, bodily, parts are destroyed.

In this light Williamson (1970:237) is wrong in claiming that Philo does not use the fire motif as 'a constituent of the parabolic warning' (which does happen in the Epistle to the Hebrews 6:8), but only as the punishment of the cities in the 'literal meaning'. In the very passage under scrutiny by Williamson (Abr 166), the destruction by fire is interpreted, not just 'literally', but allegorically as directed against four of the five human senses. Although the word 'fire' is not used here, the motif itself is present and therefore applied universally and not only to the literal cities. Moreover, the fire that rained on Sodom is explicitly allegorised elsewhere (QuaestGn 4:51) as a *warning*. Another argument against Williamson's view of the use of fire in Philonic literature is afforded by the smoke mentioned two paragraphs later (QuaestGn 4:53), which is part and parcel of the motif of destruction by fire. It is also used in an allegorical passage, where it is incorporated into a deeper meaning.

After a section on Abraham and Isaac (Abr 167-199) and its allegory (Abr 200-207), Philo comes to that part of the biblical Sodom tradition where we are told how Lot became an inhabitant of Sodom. In **De Abrahamo 204-216, 217-224** the main features of Genesis 13 are worked into an encomium of Abraham and harsh words about the character of Lot. Where Josephus regards Lot as a good man (cf below, p 102), Philo thinks he was unreliable, rebellious and moody (Abr 211; cf Sap 10:6, Jub 16:8-9). When they have to part, Abraham allows Lot to choose the land where he wants to go. Lot of course opts for the best land, i e the Sodom vicinity, but Abraham gains peace, which is better than the best land.

Allegorically, this means that the *tropoi psychès*, the characters of the soul, are like two herdsmen who control their flocks. The one is 'external' and the other is 'moral' (Abr 220-221). The conflict between the two groups takes place in the soul (Abr 222-223). This results in the lower 'external' character (represented in the text by Lot and his possessions) having to leave.

De Abrahamo 225-235, 236-244 deals with Genesis 14 and contains more of Philo's use of the Sodom and Gomorrah symbolism. The picture of a situation typical of the period of the judges, found in Genesis 14, is retained (Abr 226). The motif of the paradise-like Pentapolis region also occurs here (Abr 227), as well as the idea that its wealth led the inhabitants to their overbearing attitude (Abr 228; cf Abr 134 and Josephus, Ant 1:194). When the invading kings punish the rebellious Pentapolis, Abraham feels pity for the latter (cf Josephus, Ant 176, who even calls the Sodomites Abraham's friends). Abraham's victory is described in some detail which is comparable to the description given by Josephus (cf below, p 99). Philo ends with the Melchizedek episode and does not discuss Abraham's unwillingness to be enriched by the king of Sodom (Gn 14:21-24; he does discuss it, however, in LegAll 3:24). This may be a consequence of the demands of the allegory, where the king of Sodom stands for the sense of touch, the lowest of the senses, and Abraham stands for the *logos* which in principle cannot be of any benefit to the lower senses (see below).

The allegory of the passage develops the motif of the senses by linking them to the human passions. The four invading kings stand for the four passions, pleasure, lust, fear and sorrow, while the five Pentapolis kings stand for the five senses (Abr 236). These nine are kings since they have dominion over their respective terrains (Abr 237). The senses pay tribute to the passions in that they provide the strength for the passions, and there is peace as long as they serve the four passion kings in this way. However, when old age comes and the senses diminish, war ensues and the four passions are victorious over the five senses (Abr 239-240). According to Genesis 14:10 the kings of Sodom and Gomorrah fall into the pits in the vicinity. Philo interprets this (Abr 241) as the biblical indication that the senses of touch and taste sink lower than the others. Although it is not explicitly said, Sodom, the first of the two mentioned in the verse, must stand for the sense of touch and Gomorrah must stand for taste (as Zoar stands for sight, the senses of hearing and smell must be thought of as being represented by Admah and Zeboim). Abraham, here called 'the courteous one' (*ho asteios*, Abr 242), then intervenes on the side of the senses against the passions in order to restore democracy in the soul (i e each part should have its proper power, cf Colson [1935] 1966:118). Abraham, being the tenth leader on the scene, stands for the *logos*, which is represented by the number 10, the perfect number (1+2+3+4, cf Sacr 122). Whereas the nine kings are all corruptible, the tenth one is divine and superior to them (Abr 244).

Our second main text is Philo's **Quaestiones in Genesin Book 4.** The whole work of four books consists, as the name suggests, of a collection of questions and answers on the Book of Genesis. It follows the biblical text almost verse by verse and, because of the allegorical interpretations, has a sort of staccato effect. It is, in fact, a set of Philonic notes on the Book of Genesis. Therefore we shall discuss it as such. Much of what we have already encountered will crop up here again, and we shall avoid repetition as far as possible. Because of the organisation of the text before us, we may also keep our discussion in the form of a set of notes.

Mambre (= Mamre) is interpreted as 'from sight', obviously from the Hebrew *min* + *mar'è*, and the light of midday is coupled with Philo's theme of the importance of sight (cf Thyen 1965:2302; QuaestGn 4:1; Gn 18:1).

The relationship between the three visitors (plural) and the singular in Genesis 18 is explained as a matter of the three powers behind which God stands (QuaestGn 4:2; Gn 18:20). However, Abraham was able to recognise God in the triad (QuaestGn 4:4; Gn 18:3; cf also QuaestGn 4:6 on Gn 18:5, 4:8 on 18:6.7, and 4:25 on 18:22).

The docetic interpretation of the divine visitors' eating (cf Abr 118) is again offered (QuaestGn 4:9; Gn 18:8), and Abraham's hospitality is underlined (QuaestGn 4:20; Gn 18:16).

Sodom is taken to mean 'blindness' or 'sterility' (cf Ebr 222, where the Greek words *typhlósis* and *steirósis* are used). These stand for impiety and irrationality, but the supposed meanings of the name are obviously suggested by the blindness with which the men of Sodom were affected (Gn 19:11) and by their unnatural sexual desires (cf Abr 135 for Philo's idea of sterility in Sodom, and Heinemann [1929-1932] 1962:261-263 for his idea that sex is only meant for the begetting of children). Gomorrah is taken to mean 'measure', a name which is falsely usurped by the people of that city, since the only true measure by which all things on earth are measured is the *logos* (cf Som 2:192, where the Greek word *metron* is used). Gomorrah is, rather, the measure of wickedness (QuaestGn 4:23; Gn 18:20).

Philo thinks that Abraham wanted not only the righteous to be saved, but also the wicked for the sake of the righteous. Therefore he is an early proponent of this interpretation of Genesis 18:24-32 (QuaestGn 4:27; cf Brueggemann 1982:173-174 on the 'new arithmetic' of this passage).

In the following paragraphs (QuaestGn 4:30.33.35 on Gn 19:1-3) Lot is unfavourably contrasted with Abraham. He could not recognise God between his two potencies in the visiting triad but only recognised a diad (as can be expected of as lesser person). Neither did his hospitality compare well with that of Abraham.

The wickedness of the men of Sodom (Gn 19:5.7-8) was pederasty, which allegorically means that impure people threaten those who are self-controlled. As for Lot's abandoning his daughters to the lust of the mob, its deeper meaning is that the feminine thoughts within us, that is, the thoughts of the passions, should be abandoned in favour of the masculine thoughts, that is, the thoughts of wisdom and virtue when it is necessary for the preservation of the latter (QuaestGn 4:37.38). This allegory is not particularly unfavourable for Lot, but that does not seem to matter for Philo.

The 'law of the Sodomites' is that all beings have desire and that this is the most important thing. They are therefore regarded as hedonists in principle. In their search for satisfaction of this lust, they even tried to enter Lot's house after having been blinded (QuaestGn 4:39.41; Gn 19:9.11).

God himself did not bring about the destruction; he does good, while the angels do the destructive deeds (QuaestGn 4:42; Gn 19:12-13, cf Josephus, Ant 1:200-202a).

In the following paragraphs (QuaestGn 4:46-50) Lot's flight (Gn 19:17-22) is allegorised. Mountains are high and man must strive for higher things. Lot acknowledged his inability to do so and was accepted by God for not boasting. Still, man has to contribute to his salvation and hasten to it. The 'mountain' to which Lot must flee, is called Zoor (cf Josephus Ant 1:204: *Zoor*). This version of the name Zoar is probably related to the faulty etymology of the Hebrew ṣoʿar, which is supposed to derive from ṣûr, 'rock' (Marcus [1953] 1979:326).

The purpose of the destruction is to warn future generations (QuaestGn 4:51; Gn 19:23-24; cf Schlosser 1973:17). It was something special, since fire is by nature light and inclined to rise, while in the case of Sodom it descended. Sodom on earth stands for the opposite of the paradise of creation.

Lot's wife was not punished in the same way as Sodom because she was not guilty of the same transgression (QuaestGn 4:52; Gn 19:26). Nevertheless, she should not have looked back, neither with pleasure over the destruction of sinners, nor with sorrow for those who have been justly punished. Whereas salt is usually a symbol of preservation, it is here a symbol of barrenness (again the opposite of its nature, as was the case with descending fire). Abraham also looked on (QuaestGn 4:53; Gn 19:27.28), but he did so with piety. The allegorical meaning of the smoke seen by Abraham is that the feverish, passionate body exhales vapours like the rising smoke of destruction.

Lot was not saved for his own sake, but for that of Abraham (QuaestGn 4:54; Gn 19:29), which again plays Lot down. However, in the following paragraphs he becomes the allegorical representative of the mind, who has two daughters, 'Counsel' and 'Consent' (cf Marcus [1953] 1979:335, who refers to PostC 175, where they appear as *boulè* and *sygkatathesis*). Consent can only follow counsel and their children can only be fathered by the mind. 'Moab' expresses pride in the child of the mind, while 'Ammon' relates to the feeling of the masses, Hebrew: *'âm*, 'people' (QuaestGn 4:55-58; Gn 19:30-38).

We may not find this a negative interpretation, but it is given such a slant in **De posteritate Caini 175-177.** Here it is said that God is the one who 'raises' (*exanistèmi*), that is, who causes a family to come into existence. This may be suggested by the faulty derivation of *theos* from *tithèmi*. Therefore not the mind (represented by Lot in the text), but God is the one who brings into being. If the mind is sober, it acknowledges this, but if it is drunk and therefore full of folly, it desires to perform the creative function of God (Philo does not pay attention to the fact that Lot was oblivious of what was happening). That is why the posterity of Lot is excluded from the assembly of God (Dt 23:4).

Abraham's prayer for Sodom and the meaning of the numbers of the righteous (Gn 18:23-33) is treated in **De mutatione nominum 228, De sacrificiis Abelis et Caini 122,** and **De congressu quaerendae eruditionis gratia 109.** The first of these is found in the context of an argument, based on several issues from Genesis 17, that we should strive to do what little we can if we cannot achieve the highest (cf Colson & Whitaker [1934] 1968:139). Abraham's prayer is an example of this principle. Fifty, being the number of complete liberty (cf Lv 25:10 on the Jubilee Year which should be consecrated every fifty years), could not be attained, so he wanted the number ten, the symbol of a lower training (*paideia*), to be accepted instead for the benefit of Sodom. The same is found in the second passage (Sacr 122), where the number ten is said to be dedicated to education (*kata paideian horizón*). According to Colson and Whitaker ([1927] 1979:491-492), the association of ten with education was derived from Leviticus 27:32 which speaks of 'every tenth under the rod'. In the Septuagint the word *rhabdos* is used, which was equated with *paideia* to forge the link between 'ten' and 'education'. However, this was still asking too much, for the overwhelming evil of Sodom tipped the scales to the detriment of the inhabitants. Once again the deeper meaning of the two numbers is expounded in the third of the passages mentioned (Congr 109), this time in the context of an explicit reference by Philo to the Jubilee or 'Release' (Lv 25; Congr 108). It is added in this passage that Sodom stands for a soul barren in respect of the good and blind in respect of reason. In any event Sodom did not fulfil the minimum requirement for salvation, and that is not literally ten good people, but the minimum education in what is good. Here again we must take issue with Williamson (1970:239), according to whom sterility or barrenness is used by Philo only as part of God's punishment but not as the cause of punishment. While it is true that the motif is often used in the former sense, the latter also occurs. In the passage we have just been considering (Congr 109) Philo allegorises the barren land to mean the unfruitful soul which is consumed by fire.

The passions that attack the soul (ConfLing 21-22) are allegorically re-presented by the deluge (ConfLing 23-25), by the alliance who were Abraham's opponents when he, according to Genesis 14, came to the rescue of the Sodomites (ConfLing 26), and by the conduct of the Sodo-mites against the visiting angels. In **De confusione linguarum 27-28** the latter allegory is worked out with reference to the barrenness in wisdom and the blindness in understanding which is supposed to be hidden in the meaning of the name (Colson & Whitaker [1932] 1968:553: *kata glóttan*, referring to the name of Sodom, means that the word is obscure and needs to be explained). The mob who surrounded Lot's house really surrounded the house of the soul in order to bring disgrace to the holy thoughts (*hieroi kai hosioi logoi*) inside.

The motifs of blindness in understanding and of the holy *logoi* occur also in **De fuga et inventione 121-122, 144.** In the first case it is noteworthy that the blindness of the *logismos* is related neither to the name of Sodom nor to the blindness of the mob at Lot's house, but to Lot's wife (Gn

19:26). This is an allegory of a person who is lazy in exercising his mind and therefore looks back instead of forward. Basically the same interpretation of Lot's wife is found in **De ebrietate 164-166** where she is called 'Custom' (*synètheia*) because she looked back and was opposed to truth (her daughters 'Counsel' and 'Consent' and her husband 'Mind' also feature, as in QuaestGn 4:55-58). In **Legum allegoriae 3:213**, however, she is petrified because her turning back is taken to mean that she loved the qualities (*physeis*) which God rejected. In the second case (Fug 144) the Sodomites, blinded in understanding as they are, try to do damage to the holy *logoi* but are unable to find the entrance.

De somniis 1:85 is about the meaning of the fact that the sun was rising when Lot arrived in Zoar (Gn 19:23.24). Here the sun stands for the *logos* (cf the visitors to Lot's house just referred to; it can also be a metaphor for various other concepts, cf Klein 1962:31-33). The divine *logos* helps those who turn to him, and therefore shines forth as Lot receives his help.

The hiatus left in Philo's discussion of Genesis 14 in that he pays no attention to Abraham's refusal of the king of Sodom's proposal (Gn 14:21-24; Abr 235, 244), is filled in **Legum allegoriae 3:24, 197.** Abraham saw through the king's offer to let him take that which does not have the faculty of reason while the king himself demanded that which does have reason. Had he accepted, the king of Sodom would have been able to say that he has enriched a man whose eyes are open. The context is about the fact that good people do not accept profit from what is evil (LegAll 3:23), so Abraham's conduct serves as an example of this principle. Here Abraham stands for a person of virtue, while in Philo's corresponding treatment of Genesis 14 (Abr 244) he stands for the *logos*. In the second passage (LegAll 3:197) Philo again refers to the confrontation between Abraham and the king of Sodom. Here too he refuses to keep the horses (*hè hippos*, the translation of the Septuagint for the Hebrew *rᵉkûš*, which means 'goods' and can include cattle; cf Colson & Whitaker [1929] 1971:316). Abraham keeps God's gifts, but not that of Sodom.

Our last two passages from Philo's works concern the reference in Deuteronomy 32:32.33 to the vines of Sodom and Gomorrah. The two cities, the motifs of blindness and barrenness, and that of wine are all mentioned in **De ebrietate 222-224** and **De somniis 2:191-192.** In both cases wine is a symbol of folly. Drunkenness represents wickedness, and wickedness is barren of any good and blind to what is worthy. This fits the interpretation of the name of Sodom as 'barren' and 'blind'. So here the well-known motif of the Sodomite wasteland functions as an allegory of folly and wickedness which can be seen in drunkenness. Gomorrah as 'measure' also occurs elsewhere and has already been discussed (cf QuaestGn 4:23, p 92 above).

It is not so simple to summarise Philo's use of the Sodom and Gomorrah traditions. His multiple and variegated use of the motifs contained in these traditions is too chequered for that. Without trying to incorporate all the detail discussed above, we may, however, mention the following:

1. Philo's use of the Sodom and Gomorrah traditions is heavily determined by the fact that the Sodom Cycle is part of the Jewish Holy Scripture.

2. He knows the familiar motifs, like wickedness (especially the sexual motif and gluttony), wealth, punishment, and he concentrates a lot on the ideas of barrenness and blindness.

3. His use of these motifs is the important aspect and involves his overriding interest in the allegorical meaning of the motifs in question.

4. The over-arching theme in his exposition is that the Sodom and Gomorrah tradition becomes a textbook case of the folly of bodily lusts and passions vis-à-vis the wisdom of the mind and reason; his use of it stands in the service of an attack on hedonism and breathes the spirit of a stern Stoic-type of ethic.

5. The destruction of Sodom and Gomorrah becomes an allegory of the destruction of what is bodily as opposed to what is spiritual and lasting.

6. He uses the first part of the Sodom Cycle not only to extol the virtue of Abraham, but also to expound his own concept of God (in concentrating on the three/one phenomenon or the triad of visitors).

4.4. Flavius Josephus

The Sodom and Gomorrah tradition appears several times in both major works of Flavius Josephus (c 37 - c 100 CE). We find Sodom, the land of Sodom, or the Sodomites in three passages of De Bello Judaico, which was published about 78 CE, and in three passages of Antiquitates Judaicae, which was published about 94 CE. Two of the passages in the latter work are extended sections of Josephus's retelling of the contents of Genesis (Ant 1:169-185, roughly covering Gn 13-15, and Ant 1:194-206, roughly coinciding with the Sodom Cycle of Gn 18-19) and will therefore be discussed as units. We shall start with the older work.

Our first two references to Sodom occur in the fourth of five geographical digressions. All of these relate directly to the historical events that took place in the vicinities described, and the long ecphrasis (BJ 4:451-485) with which we are here concerned marks the end of a historical narrative (Varneda 1986:172). Therefore these digressions do not break the compositional care for which Josephus is known (cf Shutt 1961:11).

In **De Bello Judaico 4:453** the mountain range from Jericho north- and southwards is described. This is part of a description of Jericho, the plain and the Dead Sea (called Asphaltitis), which in turn is incorporated into a chapter on the final stages of Vespasian's campaign in the Jewish War. Sodom is only mentioned as the southern tip of this hill district which, according to Josephus, is barren and uninhabited. The barrenness of the Sodom vicinity is an established motif in the tradition, but in this case the whole range from Scythopolis (Bethshan; cf Thackeray [1928] 1957:133) in the north to Sodom in the south is so described. Worth noting, however, is that Sodom is associated with the southern extremities (*tón peratón*) of the Dead Sea and that this is, for Josephus, an unproblematical localisation.

Of more direct importance for Josephus's understanding of the Sodom and Gomorrah tradition is the description he gives in **De Bello Judaico 4:483-485** of Lake Asphaltitis itself. Exaggerating the proportions of the lake, Josephus claims that its southern end is Zoara, which is obviously the Zoar of the Sodom tradition and is here supposed to be a known point (cf Thackeray [1928] 1957:143 for a possible identification). The 'land of Sodom' (*Sodomitis*) is said to be adjacent to the lake, not submerged by it. Josephus explicitly says that traces of divine fire and five cities are still to be seen and probably refers to the Jebel Usdum at the southwestern end of the Dead Sea. The traditional motifs of fecundity (*karpoi*) and wealth (*periousia*), found in Genesis and Ezekiel (cf Gn 13:10, Ezk 16:49) are here presented as pertaining to the various cities of the 'land of Sodom'. Not only the city of Sodom, but the whole land, i e the Pentapolis, was guilty of impiety (*asebeia*) and was therefore destroyed. The interesting aspect here is not only that Josephus blames the whole district for impiety, but also that he presents the catastrophe as having been caused by 'thunder-bolts' or 'thunder-and-lightning' (*keraunoi*). The same is found elsewhere in his account of the catastrophe (BJ 5:566, Ant 1:203) and is a rationalisation of the rain of fire spoken of in Genesis 19:24. The destruction came about because of divine wrath (cf *asebeia* as the cause, and the 'divine fire', *theios pur*, spoken of in the following lines). Our passage is particularly interesting for the way it ends. Josephus refers to the fruit of Sodom which seems to be edible, but which dissolves into ash if plucked (Tertullian also knows about this fruit; cf below, p 130). This description fits the osher-fruit found in the vicinity (cf Thackeray [1928] 1957:145). It is here presented, together with the claim that traces of the five cities and the fire that devoured them can still be seen, as empirical proof that the stories (*mytheuomena*) about the land of Sodom are credible (BJ 4:485). Empirical proof and rational argument do not exclude 'the irrational', as Varneda (1986:188) calls it, from the work of Josephus. This also occurs elsewhere in connexion with the Sodom story (Lot's wife, Ant 1:203), and is a feature found often in his writings (cf Varneda 1986:188-200 for a discussion and examples). The description of the land of Sodom, then, serves the overall apologetic purpose of Josephus: The Jewish tradition is true. While this apology for the Jewish heritage is in keeping with what we know of the purpose of his literary activity (cf Foerster 1959:868-869), the description of the Sodomite wickedness as *asebeia* can be attributed to Josephus's religious education and Pharisaic sympathies (cf Franxman 1979:3).

In **De Bello Judaico 5:566** an incidental but significant reference to Sodom is made. If the Romans had delayed the destruction of Jerusalem any longer, it would have perished by thunder like Sodom or it would have been swallowed by the earth or overflowed by water. This is a clear reference to the deluge and probably also to the story of Korah, Dathan and Abiram who were swallowed up by the earth (Nu 16). Accordingly, we have a combination of the flood and the Sodom motifs which occurs so often that it should be regarded as a fixed traditional motif (cf Lührmann 1972:130-132), and possibly also a reference to the 'generation of the wilderness' which is associated by the rabbis with the people of the flood and those of Sodom (cf Sanh 108a, 110b). The reason for the destruction of the city is that its inhabitants were worse than those who suffered these devastations. This reminds us of Ezekiel, who also uses the Sodom tradition to compare Jerusalem *in malam partem* (cf Ezk 16:48). On the interpretation of the fire from heaven as thunder, see the discussion of the previous paragraph.

Our first extended text from Josephus's other main work is **Antiquitates Judaicae 1:169-185.** This is an abridged version of Genesis 13-15 (cf Franxman 1979:286). Josephus begins by telling how Lot separated from Abraham and chose the Jordan valley 'not far from the city of Sodom' (Ant 1:170). Where Genesis 13:12 makes Lot move gradually to Sodom, Josephus presents a picture of Lot who lives in the vicinity of the city, which agrees with his conception of 'Sodom' as the whole land of Sodom, *Sodomitis*. At this juncture Josephus refers to the erstwhile prosperity of the land and its subsequent destruction 'by the will of God', thereby implying that the destruction was necessary (at this point Gn 13:13 refers to the wickedness of the Sodomites). However, he refers the reader to what follows for an elaboration (cf par 194).

Continuing to the equivalent of Genesis 14, Josephus informs us about his view of the political dispensation obtaining in Sodom. When the Assyrians (according to Josephus they were the invaders from the east, Gn 14:1) were masters of Asia, the country of Sodom was ruled by five kings (equivalent names of the kings of the five cities mentioned in Gn 14:2 are given). Each king had his own *moirai*, which can mean a division of an army or a part of a state. The latter has preference here, for the author is referring to their country and not (yet) to their war against the invaders. This would account for the fact that the Pentapolis or the whole district of Sodom appears in Josephus's works as a unit (cf BJ 4:483). In this way, also, he can successfully abridge the material as it is no longer necessary to mention the names of the cities or to differentiate between them. The dominant name in the tradition, Sodom, becomes an umbrella designation of the region as a whole.

The account of the Assyrian invasion follows Genesis 14 in presenting a picture of a typical story from the Book of Judges. The invaders encamp in the Valley of Bitumen Pits, but the local kings, who, according to the Genesis version, fall into the pits, are spared that ignominy by Josephus. Instead he promises to shortly give a description of Lake Asphaltitis which has come in the place of the valley with its pits. However, he does not do this and his readers have to turn to the passage discussed above (BJ 4:483-485; cf Thackeray [1930] 1961:85) to find such a description. Lot is presented as an ally (*symmachos*, par 175) of the Sodomites and not as a true member of the wicked community, which is consistent with the fact that Josephus is sympathetic to him (cf below). It is remarkable that Abraham is said to have felt compassion for the Sodomites when he heard that they had been routed. It is even more notable that they are not only called his neighbours (*geitnióntoi*), but also his friends (*philoi*; par 176). In this way Abraham's merit is stressed (cf his plea for the Sodomites in par 199). Some details about the way in which Abraham gained the upper hand against the Assyrians are given (cf Philo, Abr 233-234; Thackeray [1930] 1961:86). In conclusion Abraham refuses to be enriched by the king of Sodom, as he does in Genesis 14:22-24. (It is interesting that Philo, Abr 233-235, omits this detail, but that he does mention it in LegAll 3:24.)

The second extended passage is **Antiquitates Judaicae 1:194-206.** It can be called Josephus's main passage on Sodom since it is his version of what I have called the Sodom Cycle (Gn 18-19). Franxman (1979:141) is right in stating that the natural unit found in Genesis 18-19 is made 'even tighter' by Josephus. I would also agree with him that it is best to consider Josephus's narrative according to its own structure and not according to that of Genesis. It consists of six sections:

A. The wickedness of the Sodomites and God's resolution to destroy them (par 194-195).

B. The visit of the angels and the promise of a child (par 196-198).

C. Abraham's grief for the Sodomites and his plea for them (par 199).

D. The visit of the angels to Lot and their experience with the crowd of Sodom (par 200-202a).

E. Lot's flight from Sodom and the destruction of the land (par 202b-204).

F. Lot's daughters and their progeny (par 205-206).

Like Franxman (1979:142, 144), I arrive at three sections parallel to Genesis 18 and three parallel to Genesis 19, but my description of the sections differs. In the second section of his portrayal of the stucture, Franxman curiously seems to find a break at 'the laughter of Sarah'. He also describes the structure 'according to the pace set by Genesis', which is just what he says we should not do. The outline given above already shows that Josephus has compressed the narrative into a unit about Sodom in that he opens with a section about the wickedness of the Sodomites (A) and not, as the biblical story does, with Abraham's hospitality towards his three guests (B). Further, the fourth section of the biblical narrative is omitted (cf above, p 15, where I have designated this section, Gn 19:27-29, as B') as well as a statement to the effect that Lot was saved for Abraham's sake (Gn 19:29). This squares with the tendency of Josephus not to play down Lot *vis-à-vis* Abraham, while Lot is criticised often in pseudepigraphic and Rabbinic literature (but sometimes defended; cf above, p 77-78, where Sap 10:6 and Jub 16:8-9 are cited as examples of the opposing views; references to mainly Rabbinic examples are given by Ginzberg 1925:240, n 171).

Our passage begins by giving the approximate date for the origin of the Sodomites' wickedness. When Abraham was circumcised at the age of ninety-nine, the Sodomites began to show insolence (*hybris*) towards people and impiety (*asebeia*) towards God (*hybristai, asebeis*, par 194). Josephus suggests that this stemmed from their great numbers and wealth (cf Philo, Abr 134, PRE 25, Sanh 109a on the wealth of the Sodomites). The manifestation of this wickedness was that they became *misoxenoi*, haters of strangers. This motif is copiously attested in the Rabbinic literature and naturally connected with the Sodomites' parsimony (cf Ginzberg 1925:237-238, n 155). In the opening section of our passage we therefore have a logical explanation of the Sodomite sin: Wealth breeds parsimony, which leads to the hatred of strangers who may endanger their wealth, and this in turn leads to cruelty towards strangers. This train of thought can be linked to several elements in the biblical tradition of Sodom and Gomorrah: Abraham receives strangers kindly; Lot does the same; the Sodomites violate the right of the strangers. The emphasis on Abraham's hospitality and on that of Lot (which Josephus develops carefully in par 200) is contrasted by the motif of violation of the ancient custom by the Sodomites. Their treatment of the strangers, expressed as it is in sexual terms, is therefore, according to Josephus, a manifestation of social violence (cf below, p 102 on *bia*). In view of the fact that the wealth of Sodom is the root of this social violence, we are entitled to call Josephus's concept of the wickedness of the Sodomites socio-economic violence. This means that Josephus interpreted this aspect of the Sodom and Gomorrah tradition essentially as I have done (cf above, p 37). The same would then also have to be said of the rest of the Jewish tradition where the motifs of wealth and xenophobia occur in connexion with Sodom. All of this would mean that the Sodom Cycle in Genesis, the prophets with their social message, and a large part of the Jewish tradition have fundamentally the same view of the wickedness of Sodom (and Gomorrah). The result is, according to Josephus, that God resolves to devastate the city and the whole land so that nothing would be left of its previous fruitfulness.

Section B of our passage is about the visit of three angels to Abraham at Mambre (MT: *mamrê*; LXX: *Mambre*). Josephus is careful never to suggest that it was God who came to Abraham, which means that an important aspect of the Genesis narrative is eliminated by him (just the opposite applies to Philo who exploits the oscillation of singular and plural in Gn 18; cf Abr 132, QuaestGn 4:6.8.9.11.12). This may be ascribed to his apologetic purpose, but it also agrees with the tendency to eliminate anthropomorphism when speaking of God, which is so typical of Jewish texts. Abraham is presented as killing and cooking the calf himself, while Genesis 18:7 (which is ambiguous in both the Masoretic Text and the Septuagint) allows that a servant had at least a part in the preparation. This has the effect of enhancing Abraham's hospitality, which becomes important later when it is to be said whence Lot's hospitality is derived (cf par 200). The angels only appear to be eating the meal, which is a 'docetic' interpretation of Genesis 18:8 (Thackeray [1930] 1961:97) and is often found (cf TgNeof Gn 18:8, Philo, Abr 118, BerR 48:14, QohR 3:14, as opposed to Tertullian, CarnChrist 3:41; cf below, p 131; cf Ginzberg 1900:108, who cites Theodoret's 'docetic' interpretation *hós óphthèsan ephagon*). During the meal the angels enquire about Sarah (*Sarra*) and declare that they will return 'one day' when Sarah will have become a mother. Josephus has Sarah smile instead of laugh by herself (Gn 18:12), which is the cue for the angels to reveal their true identity. One had the function of announcing the birth of Abraham's son and the other two were to destroy Sodom (there is no question of investigating the rumours about Sodom and Gomorrah, Gn 18:21). The division of functions is well known in Jewish literature (Franxman 1979:144; cf TgJ1, TgJ2, TgNeof on Gn 18:2, Philo, Abr 142-146, BerR 50:2, BMez 86b). It may be argued that the *three* visitors of Genesis 18, interpreted as angels, and the *two* angels of Genesis 19 could give rise to the inference that there was a division of functions between them, but it cannot be said that this aspect of Jewish angelology is based only on this text (Philo gives a completely different interpretation in QuaestGn 4:30).

The third section of the passage (par 199) abridges the agonising quest for justice in Genesis 18:23-33. Abraham feels grief even for the wicked Sodomites. The biblical dialogue is reduced to one sentence about a prayer of Abraham addressed to God and not to one of the company of three (for they are angels and cannot be addressed in prayer), and one sentence about there not even being ten good people in Sodom. Significantly, Josephus adds: 'So Abraham kept quiet (*hèsychazen*)' – thus neutralising the daring tenacity with which the Abraham of Genesis 18 keeps on talking back to God.

In the fourth section (par 200-202a) the hospitality of Lot is praised. He was 'exceedingly' (*lian*) kind to strangers, a virtue taught him by Abraham while they were still together (cf BerR 50:4, PRE 25). In this way the motif of hospitality in Genesis 19 is linked to that in Genesis 18, which contributes to the moulding of the two halves of the Sodom story even more tightly together. Extolling the virtue of Lot also places Josephus firmly in the camp of those who disagree with the tradition that he was bad (cf above, pp 78, 90). Josephus, in describing the outrage of the mob against the angels, prudently suggests the sexual motif by pointing out twice that the young men had a fair appearance, and by telling of Lot's offer of his daughters to satisfy the lust (*epithymia*) of the mob in their stead. But it is clear that the sexual outrage is, for Josephus, only the outward manifestation of the basic wickedness of the Sodomites, viz violence and insolence. Therefore he actually uses the terms *bia* and *hybris* to describe their conduct towards the young men (cf above, pp 100-101). God, and not the visitors (Gn 19:10), blinds the Sodomites.

In the penultimate section the pace is accelerated and nothing of the tension created by the technique of retardation in the biblical narrative is to be found here. First we hear of Lot's flight (par 202b), then about the destruction (par 203a), and then again about the flight (par 203b-204). It is said that God threw a thunderbolt on the city, that the inhabitants were burnt, and that the whole land was similarly destroyed. This agrees with what we have found in other Josephus texts (BJ 4:483-485, 5:566; cf above, pp 97-98). Lot's wife was turned into a pillar of salt because she turned round continually, not just once. So God cannot be accused of being too severe in punishing her for one little lapse. Josephus insists on having seen the pillar himself, and so adds to the credibility of the Jewish tradition. The reference to Lot's miserable life in Zóór (Zoar) leads to the final section.

Here the tradition of Lot's union with his daughters is told with a sympathetic slant. Josephus says that the girls thought the whole of humanity was dead and that they therefore acted in good faith to preserve the human race. He also stresses that Lot knew nothing of what was happening and thereby exonerates him in case some reader were to take offence at the girls' conduct. Josephus ends the narrative with a concluding formula (par 206).

Among the Sodom passages of Josephus especially this one testifies to the 'careful composition and sustained effort' (Shutt 1961:11) found in his work. It is also an ideal example of Josephus's philosophy of history, to which he himself refers (Ant 1:23-24), that humans should strive to participate in God's perfect virtue and that God punishes people who do not accept this (cf Shutt 1961:12). As Josephus wants his readers to examine the whole book in this light (Ant 1:24), we are obliged to do so with the Sodom story. The result is that we must declare that Josephus remained true to his philosophy of history and that this story is an excellent illustration, if not *the* illustration of his fundamental historical premise.

Antiquitates Judaicae 5:81 is relevant to our purpose in that it refers to the Dead Sea as the 'Lake of Sodom' (*Sodomitidos limnè*). The context is the division of the land under Joshua, and in the appropriate place (Jos 15:2) the Septuagint speaks of the 'Salt Sea' (*thalassè tès halykès*). Josephus must refer to the southern end of the Dead Sea (Thackeray & Marcus [1934] 1958:38).

By way of summary we may say the following of Josephus's use of the Sodom and Gomorrah traditions:

1. His dependence on the Genesis story is obvious, and he welds both halves of it even more tightly into one Sodom story by beginning and ending his version of Genesis 18-19 with 'the Sodomites'.

2. Josephus knows the familiar motifs of the Sodom and Gomorrah traditions (wickedness, punishment, fruitfulness, wasteland), but his use of them is noteworthy in at least two general respects.

3. First, his interpretation of the wickedness in socio-economic terms is clear and contributes to our understanding of this element in the biblical as well as in later Jewish Sodom texts.

4. Second, his rationalising of the Jewish tradition (lightning, empirical

103

'proof') reveals just as clearly the pro-Jewish sympathies of his Pharisaic background and the apologetic function of his writing.

5. Josephus's handling of the Sodom and Gomorrah tradition amiably expresses his philosophy of history – punishment for those who do not strive after God's virtue.

4.5. Rabbinic literature

Our last category of Jewish literature is the vast corpus of Rabbinic writings. Especially two problems related to each other arise here. First, it is extremely difficult to be exhaustive in the absence of complete concordances and precise indices to the material. Second, the corpus is so huge that anyone attempting to work through the whole spectrum would do well to keep modesty in mind. I therefore stress that what goes for Louis Ginzberg, the best guide in a project such as the present one, goes for all studies of this nature. Having referred to the 'luxuriant abundance of the material', he says: 'I can therefore claim completeness for my work only as to content' (Ginzberg 1909:xiv).

What follows here, is an attempt in this spirit to gather those passages relevant to our topic from the Rabbinic literature and to determine how the Sodom and Gomorrah traditions are used there. An endeavour has been made to be as complete as possible, and I hope that I can claim that the material brought together is representative of the use made of these traditions in the Rabbinic current of Jewish thought. As I have explained in the introductory chapter (cf above, p 13), we shall go no further than the Talmudic period. The discussion will also be kept as brief as possible in order not to disturb the balance of the study.

Apart from the many shorter and incidental references to Sodom (and Gomorrah), the literature that now interests us contains two basic texts concerning Sodom. Both are extended texts and focus on the tradition itself. The first is found in the Midrash Rabbah, which is obviously important because it comments on the biblical text (in our case the Book of Genesis) verse by verse and is therefore bound to pay much attention to the Sodom Cycle. The second fundamental text is the Talmudic narrative in Sanhedrin 109a-b, the elements of which are found in several parallel passages of Rabbinic literature (cf TSot 3:11-12, Mek Ex 15:1, WayyR 4:1, 7:6, BemR 9:24, Midr Qoh 2:2). We shall use these two texts as the framework for our discussion and refer to others where appropriate. (In keeping with English parlance I use the title 'Rabbi' for both Palestinian and Babylonian authorities.)

In **Bereshit Rabbah 41:3-10** the separation between Abram and Lot is discussed. Lot is not seen in a very favourable light. He was allowed to accompany Abram, he was saved by Abram when the Sodomites were taken captive by the invading kings, and he was saved from Sodom because of Abram. For these reasons his descendants should have treated Israel kindly instead of badly (BerR 41:3). However, good can come from bad, since David was 'found' in Sodom, that is, King David was descended from the inhabitant of Sodom, Lot, via Ruth the Moabitess (BerR 41:4; cf 50:10). The strife (*rîb*) between the herdsmen of Abram and of Lot had much to do with the fact that Abram was so careful as to have his own cattle muzzled, while Lot did not take the precaution. In the ensuing argument it was Abram who offered Lot the choice of where to go (BerR 41:5-6). Lot's 'lifting his eyes' (*nś' 'èt 'ênayim*) to look at the land already betrays his immoral character, because he looked up with sexual desire (like Potiphar's wife, Gn 39:7, in whose case the same expression is used). In going to Sodom he renounced both Abram and the God of Abram. According to Rabbi (*c* 135 - 193 CE; Strack [1931] 1969:118), Sodom was the worst city of all, for which reason the wickedness of Sodom became proverbial (cf Ket 103a, Erub 49a, BB 12b). But according to Rabbi Jose (*c* 150 CE; Strack [1931] 1969:115) the other cities of the plain were just as bad (cf TShab 7:23; Philo, Abr 165, regards Zoar as the best among them). At this point an interesting variation should be noted. In Zohar 1:108a it is said that Lot was accepted in Sodom because of the esteem in which Abram, his kinsman, was held there (cf Josephus, Ant 1:176, who calls the Sodomites Abram's friends). However, there is also a tradition that God was angry at Abram for not making Lot cling to God as he made other people do (BerR 41:8).

The story of Abram's involvement in the campaign of the four eastern kings against the Pentapolis (Gn 14) is interpreted in **Bereshit Rabbah 42-43**. The invading kings are taken to mean Babylonia, Greece, Media and the wicked power of Rome. Abram is said to have become a great man because of the conflict of the world powers among themselves (BerR 42:4). The Pentapolis is evaluated negatively in that the five names in question are interpreted as follows (BerR 42:5): *bèra'* (king of Sodom) represents *bèn ra'* (bad son); *birša'* (king of Gomorrah) signifies *bèn râšâ'* (wicked son); *šin'âb* (king of Admah) stands for *šo'eb mammôn* (collector of money); *šèm'ebèr* (king of Zeboim) is taken to be *śâm 'ebèr* (he made wings, he flew away); *bèla'* (the city identified with Zoar, Gn 14:2) signifies that its inhabitants were swallowed up (*nitball'û*). The latter interpretation does not tally with the fact that this city was spared the catastrophe for Lot's sake. The king of Zeboim's name refers to the flight spoken of in Genesis 14, while the other three names reflect the tradition of the wickedness of the Pentapolis. *šo'eb mammôn* represents the motif of wealth so often found in the Sodom and Gomorrah traditions, and its association with the other two names suggests the injustice by means of which the wealth was come by (cf the Targum Onqelos on Gn 13:13, where the same motif is explicitly found: 'The men of Sodom were evil [*bîšîn*] in their wealth [*bᵉmâmônhôn*]'; in the Targum Pseudo-Jonathan the verse also contains this motif). Another well-known motif, that of fecundity, is also present in our passage. The Valley of Siddim is regarded as having been populated by all kinds of fruit trees. This paradise was terminated when, at the time of the destruction of the valley, the Jordan was blocked and the Dead Sea formed (BerR 42:5).

Lot was captured together with his possessions because he chose to live in Sodom, which is taken to match Proverbs 13:20 ('He who walks with the wise will become wise, but the companion of fools will be harmed'; BerR 42:7). He was eventually saved together with his fellow Sodomites by Abram. This was, of course, achieved with the help of God (BerR 43:3) but other sources say that Abram was helped by angels (Sanh 96a, PRE 27; cf Ginzberg 1909:231-232). This is an important passage since it contains the idea of proselytism (BerR 43:4). The captive adults were returned to their former station, but Abram kept the children, who became proselytes and renounced the wickedness of their Sodomite fathers. This is interpreted by Rabbi Judah in terms of Ezekiel 7:24, that even the worst of the *goyyîm* can be 'brought' to become proselytes. While the king of Sodom does not show the proper respect to his saviour (BerR 43:5), Abram swears to take nothing from him, not even a thread or a latchet. Rabbi Abba ben Mammel (fourth century CE; Strack [1931] 1969:126; Bacher [1899] 1965:530-532) relates this to Abram's attitude to the Sodomite children: He will teach them the Torah about *ṣîṣit* (Nu 15:38) and *yᵉbâmâ* (Dt 25:9) (BerR 43:9).

Bereshit Rabbah 48-49 covers the story of the visitors in Genesis 18. We shall only concentrate on those motifs that are relevant to our present purpose. It is suggested that God is recognised. No oscillation between singular and plural is exploited (BerR 48:10; cf the biblical text and Philo, Abr 131-132). Abraham's visitors tell him explicitly that they do not eat or drink (BerR 48:11), but this stands in some tension with the docetic interpretation given somewhat further on where they *pretend* to eat (BerR 48:12; cf Philo, Abr 118, QuaestGn 4:9). The second part of Genesis 18, which is directly concerned with Sodom and Gomorrah, is interpreted in chapter 49. In the opinion of Rabbi Jochanan (c 180-279 CE; on his high old age cf Strack [1931] 1969:121-122; Bacher [1892] 1965:205-339) the wickedness of the generation of the flood and that of the Sodomites are basically the same (BerR 49:5; cf Rabbi Jochanan's views on the former generation's sin of violence in Sanh 108a and the opinion that neither group has a share in *hâ'olâm habbâ'*, Mishnah Sanh 10:3).

The implication of Genesis 18:20-21, that God was at first uninformed about the state of affairs in Sodom, is circumvented by the interpretation of Rabbi Abba ben Kahana (end of the third and beginning of the fourth centuries CE; Strack [1931] 1969:126; Bacher [1896] 1965:475-512) (BerR 49:6). According to him, God, upon receiving the complaint (cry) about the wickedness of the Sodomites, first gave them the opportunity to repent and decided to punish them if they do not (*'im lô'*). This is also found in the Targum Neofiti on Gn 18:21, where God is prepared to regard their sins which are known to him as if he did not know them (*kid⁽e⁾lâ' yâda'at*), and in the Targum Pseudo-Jonathan on this verse, where God is prepared to regard the people as innocent if they repent. It also occurs in the Targum Onqelos on Genesis 6:3, which suggests that the possibility of repentance and forgiveness is a fixed element in the tradition of divine punitive action (cf Ginzberg 1900:108-109, who quotes Aphraates to the effect that God wanted the angels to bring the Sodomites to repentance; Schlosser 1973:18-19; also the discussion above, pp 76-77 on Ben Sira, and below). So the tradition must be at least three centuries older than Rabbi Abba. His interpretation is augmented by a haggadah, attributed to Rabbi Levi (late third and beginning of the fourth centuries CE; Strack [1931] 1969:124; Bacher [1896] 1965:296-436), about two girls in Sodom. The one was pale as a result of hunger and the other exchanged her bucket of flour for the starving girl's bucket of water. When the Sodomites found this out, they burned the kind girl alive. Therefore the biblical text says, '*her* cry', not '*their* cry'. The midrash is developed from two words in the text of Genesis 18:20-21 and not one only (cf Mulder 1970:1-38, who points out three expressions in the biblical text to which the haggadah is variously attached). First, there is a play on the 'great' (*rabbâ*) cry over Sodom and the word for 'girl', *rîbâ*. The words of verse 20, *za'⁽a⁾qat s⁽e⁾dom wa'⁽a⁾morâ kî rabbâ*, are then read, *za'⁽a⁾qat s⁽e⁾dom wa'⁽a⁾morâ kî rîbâ*: 'The cry of Sodom and Gomorrah because of the girl'. The second foothold for the haggadah is the third person feminine singular suffix attached to *za'⁽a⁾qâ* where one would expect a third person masculine plural (as some textual witnesses indeed attest). This kind of wickedness went on even for the 25 years preceding the destruction, during which God gave the Sodomites ample seismic warning without bringing them to repent. The story is an example of the cruelty of the Sodomites, which manifests as social oppression and stems from their gluttony and selfishness (for the parallel in Sanh 109b, cf below, p 115).

Abraham's intercession for Sodom (BerR 49:8-14; cf 39:6 and its parallel in WayyR 10:1) is not effective because there are no righteous people in Sodom. This is the opinion of Rabbi Jochanan, based on the spelling of *ṣaddîqim* with reference to Sodom. The word is always spelled defectively when associated with Sodom (cf Gn 18:24.26.28, where the *yod* of the final syllable is lacking). This indicates that even their righteousness is defective (BerR 49:9). As to the question why Abraham stopped at the number ten (Gn 18:32), three answers are given: Ten is the minimum required for a prayer service of which Sodom is in need; eight are not enough to avoid the catastrophe, as shown by the fact that the eight people in Noah's ark were not enough to avoid the deluge (Gn 6:18); Abraham thought there would be ten good people, viz Lot, his wife, his four daughters (*sic*; according to this strand of tradition he had four; cf Ginzberg 1900:109, who quotes Ephraem and Jerome to show that the Christian fathers also knew this tradition) and their husbands (BerR 49:13).

The exposition of Genesis 19 (BerR 50-51) begins with the problems of the 'angels' in Genesis 18 and 19. One angel does not perform more than one function, and the reason why there are now (Gn 19:1) only two left, is that Michael, who had brought the good news of a child for Sarah, has in the meantime departed. Gabriel was to destroy Sodom and Raphael was to rescue Lot (BerR 50:2). A variant of this tradition is found in Baba Mezia 86b, where Raphael is seen as the healer of Abraham after the latter's circumcision, while Michael accompanied Gabriel to Sodom without taking part in the destruction (cf Shab 67a, where the two angels are called Sharlai and Amarlai in an incantation). Various explanations are given for the fact that the three are called 'men' in Genesis 18 and 'angels' in Genesis 19. One of these is that they appeared as men while the Shechinah was above them, but as angels as soon as the Shechinah departed. This shows that the question of who the visitors to Abraham exactly were, was answered by using the concept of the Shechinah.

Lot was sitting in the gate of Sodom when the angels arrived. That indicates that he was the chief judge (cf also the verb *špṭ* in Gn 19:9). The other judges of Sodom were perverters of justice, as one was called (*mazlê dînâ*; the names are mostly puns on their wickedness and have been preserved in various forms – *šèrèk, šarqar, šaqrûray, šaqrûrâ, zabnak, kazban, zayyâpî, zayyâpay, mânôn*, and *qalla pandar*; cf Sanh 109b, Ginzberg 1909:246-247). Lot offered the angels hospitality, a virtue he had learnt from Abraham when he was still with him (BerR 50:4). The agreement among the Sodomites to subject all strangers to homosexual mob rape and then to rob their money (BerR 50:7; a tradition ascribed to Rabbi Bebai, *c* 320 CE; Strack [1931] 1969:126; Bacher [1899] 1965:667-669) was undermined by Lot in that he tried to prevent the Sodomites to assault his guests. This, together with the fact that the mob call out disapprovingly that he wants to 'keep playing judge' (Gn 19:9: *yišpoṭ šâpôṭ*), provides the biblical basis for the haggadah that Lot was the chief judge.

The angels were punished by God for saying, '*We* are about to destroy this place' (Gn 19:13), either because they revealed God's secret about Sodom (Rabbi Nachman, *c* 329 CE? Strack [1931] 1969:127) or because of the overbearing nature of their utterance (Rabbi Chama ben Chanina, third century CE; Strack [1931] 1969:123; Bacher [1892] 1965:447-476) (BerR 50:9). At this point (BerR 50:10) the same is said about David's origin from Sodom as in the exposition of Genesis 13:6 (BerR 41:4; cf above, p 105).

Lot still lingered because of the wealth he possessed in the city. Several examples of the motif in the Old Testament are mentioned, viz that riches can lead to destruction. Thus the well-known motif of the wealth of Sodom is here applied to Lot and generalised with reference to Ecclesiastes 5:12 (BerR 50:11). When Lot is eventually saved, it is not because of his own merit, but because of Abraham's. In fact, Abraham is so much more meritorious than Lot that the latter cannot even escape to the mountains (Gn 19:19) to live near so good a man.

Genesis 19:22-23 is interpreted to mean that the destruction took place on the sixteenth of Nisan when the sun as well as the moon are visible, because both the sun and the moon were worshipped in Sodom (BerR 50:12).

The destruction itself is interpreted in the first half of the next chapter (BerR 51:1-6). Genesis 19:23-24 is related to Psalm 58:9 by reading *himṭîr* (v 24) as a perfect tense: 'The sun rose when Lot came to Zoar, and the Lord *had* caused brimstone and fire from the Lord, from heaven, to rain on Sodom and Gomorrah'. Accordingly, the cities were destroyed before sunrise, which makes the link with Psalm 58:9 possible: A woman's miscarriage that 'does not see the sun' (i e never lives, cf Ecc 6:3-5) can be interpreted to refer to an abortion carried out at night by an adulterous woman for fear of being found out (cf Pes 93b for another interpretation of the rising sun in Gn 19:23). Therefore the demise of Sodom and Gomorrah is likened to the result of illicit sexual behaviour, which comments on the sexual aspect of their sins (BerR 51:1; cf Qid 70a).

The rain of fire and brimstone is also interpreted by means of the typical Rabbinic techniques. Rabbi Abin (fourth century CE; Strack [1931] 1969:128; Bacher [1899] 1965:653) compared the fire and brimstone (Gn 19:24) to a woman baking bread in an oven. Her own child takes a loaf with her permission and another child removes coals without being stopped. The former is God's own children who wanted bread and was granted it in a rain of bread (Ex 16:4), and the latter is the people of Sodom and Gomorrah who wanted fire and was granted it in a rain of fire. Freedman (1951:444-445) infers from this comparison that Sodom wanted the coals to injure others. This is probably correct because the comparison obviously intends to say that the people of Sodom and Gomorrah asked for what they got. As Israel asked for bread (Ex 16:2-3) and were given it, so Sodom and Gomorrah asked for fire and were given it. It can only be taken *in malam partem*. According to Rabbi Chanina ben Pazzi nothing evil descends from above, which, according to Freedman (1951:446) means that the wickedness of Sodom and Gomorrah was so great that in this case an exception was made (BerR 51:3).

The root *hpk*, often associated with Sodom and Gomorrah in the Old Testament (Dt 29:22, Is 13:19, Am 4:11, Jr 49:18, 50:40; cf above, pp 60-61, 65-66), is also attended to in the midrash (BerR 51:4). Rabbi Shemuel ben Nachman (third century CE; Strack [1931] 1969:124; Bacher [1892] 1965:477-551) interpreted the overthrow of the cities in the light of Job 28:9, where God is said in the parallelism to overturn (*hpk*) a rock/ mountains. From this can be inferred that Sodom and the other four cities of the Pentapolis were built on one rock (cf the singular *hallâmîš* in Job 28:9) and were overturned by the angel (*sc* Gabriel). The fact that the plants were also destroyed (Gn 19:25, *ṣèmaḥ hâʾᵃdâmât*, is interpreted to the effect that the barrenness of the region extends even to the atmosphere of the Sodom vicinity. For, according to Rabbi Jehoshua ben Levi (first half of the third century CE; Strack [1931] 1969:120; Bacher [1892] 1965:124-194), the rain that falls over Sodom, when collected and used for irrigation elsewhere, does not promote the growth of plants.

The flight of Lot and his family is briefly treated in the following paragraphs (BerR 51:5-7). Lot's wife became a pillar of salt because she betrayed the presence of their visitors by asking her neighbours for some salt to serve to the guests (BerR 51:5, cf 50:4; cf Ginzberg 1909:254). A good word, however, is found for Lot. He was saved because 'God remembered Abraham' (Gn 19:29). This is taken to imply that God remembered something that Lot had done for Abraham. The good thing done by Lot is inferred from the fact that Scripture says nothing about Lot objecting to the lie told by Abram when he claimed to be Sarai's brother (cf Gn 12:10-20). This happened before their parting and therefore Lot must have known about it. Somewhat ironically, therefore, it is counted in Lot's favour that he covered up a lie, while he is generally not judged very favourably (BerR 41:3-7, cf p 105; also Jub 16:8-9 as opposed to Sap 10:6; cf above, pp 78, 83, 92; further references given by Ginzberg 1925:240, n 171). The fact that Genesis 19:29 says that Lot was saved *mittôk hahᵃpêkâ*, is interpreted by Rabbi Shemuel ben Nachman to imply that Lot lived in all of the cities at various times because all were part of the *hᵃpêkâ*, while others were of the opinion that he had vested interests in the other four cities. Therefore Lot is regarded as having had a part in the wealth of Sodom.

The last paragraphs of the chapter are devoted to Lot in the cave. First David's prayer when he entered the cave, that God should not destroy (*'al taš ḥet*, Ps 57:1), is associated with the fact that earlier a similar prayer was answered for others, viz Lot and his daughters (BerR 51:7). This reference makes sense in the context, because Rabbi Shemuel's opinion about the offspring of Lot is quoted next (BerR 51:8). The girls thought that nobody but themselves survived a worldwide catastrophe (a haggadah also known to the Christian fathers; cf Ginzberg 1900:110-111, who quotes Ephraem, Ie 72B, to this effect) and wanted to preserve 'seed' (*zèra'*, Gn 19:32). According to Rabbi Shemuel the choice of the word *zèra'* has a deeper meaning and refers to the Messiah. The Messiah will be descended from David, David was descended from Ruth, and Ruth, as a Moabitess, in turn was descended from Lot through his elder daughter. The messianic significance is further underlined by the opinion of Rabbi Jehudah ben Shimon (fourth century CE; Strack [1931] 1969:129, Bacher [1899] 1965:160-220) concerning the wine given to Lot. Since Joel 4:18 says that the mountains will drip of wine 'in that day' (*bayyôm hahû'*), the drinking of wine in a cave on a mountain must have a special significance. 'That day' refers to the coming of the Messiah. Now, because of the fruitfulness of the land, the Sodomites had an abundance of wine which they hid in caves. This is how the girls got hold of wine, and so the whole episode becomes a pointer to the time of the Messiah. Even in the midst of catastrophe, punishment and misery the rabbis find the seed of hope for a glorious future. What Rudolph (1966:218) has said, in the context of the Sodom and Gomorrah tradition, of Hosea 11:9, should be adapted for the concluding paragraphs of the interpretation of the Sodom story in the Midrash Rabbah: 'Hier ist Evangelium im Midrasch'.

Our next major Rabbinic text on Sodom is found in the Babylonian Talmud, **Sanhedrin 109a-b.** The passage on Sodom begins with the declaration that the generation of Sodom has no part in the world to come, as the generation of the flood (Sanh 108a), the generation of the dispersion (Sanh 109a) and the generation of the wilderness (Sanh 110b) likewise have no part in the world to come. In all four cases an overbearing attitude is obvious from their actions (explicitly called so in the first case, Sanh 108a, and in the third, Sanh 109a). Rabbi Jehudah (†299 CE; Strack [1931] 1969:125) analysed the wickedness of the Sodomites into four types. The first is bodily sin, in other words sexual immorality, which is derived from Genesis 39:9 where the term *hârâ'â*, referring to sexual misdemeanour, occurs. This is equated to *râ'îm* in Genesis 13:13, which refers to the great sins of Sodom. The second type is sin with money, which is derived from Deuteronomy 15:9, where it is said that it will be reckoned as sin (*ḥeṭ'*) to someone who denies financial help to the poor. This is linked to the same root (*ḥaṭṭâ'îm*) used in Genesis 13:13 as a description of the Sodomites. The Sodomites were also guilty of blasphemy, which is derived not from another text, but from *lyhwh* in Genesis 13:13 itself, because this shows that their sins were directed against God. The fourth type of wickedness is bloodshed, which is derived from the fact that the word *mᵉ'od* in Genesis 13:13 is also used in 2 Kings 21:16, where it is stated that Manasseh 'shed innocent blood exceedingly (*harbê mᵉ'od*)'. These four types are also found in the Targum Pseudo-Jonathan on Genesis 13:13: The men of Sodom were wicked in their wealth (*bᵉmâmônhôn*), they offended in their bodies (*bᵉgawyatᵉhôn*), they shed innocent blood, and they rebelled against God by practising foreign worship. The first two types occur in the Targum Onqelos (Gn 13:13), while the Targum Neofiti mentions three (revealing their nakedness and shedding of innocent blood [cf the margin, *dâm zakkay*], plus practising foreign worship). This suggests that Rabbi Jehudah's four 'sins of Sodom' existed as a group at least a century earlier than his time (the third century CE), although we cannot be precise in this.

Once again we see that the socio-economic aspect is prominent in the interpretation of the Sodom and Gomorrah tradition. Two of the four types can be classified as such, and this aspect of Sodomite wickedness is stressed in both the Talmud and the targumim. This is essentially the same emphasis as that found in the Sodom Cycle, the prophets and the other Jewish corpuses that we have studied. For these reasons we can agree with Bowker (1969:190-191) who, in his discussion of Pseudo-Jonathan Genesis 13:13, states that 'the essential nature of the offence was that the natural order was inverted or reversed'. However, in my opinion this is not saying enough and should be specified further. The inversion of the natural order is essentially anti-social. That is why the biblical text itself uses the motif of inversion of the sexual order, notably to express the motif of inversion of the social order of hospitality. The first is an aspect of the second, not *vice versa* (cf above, p 37). This has been rightly recognised in the Jewish tradition reflected in the targumim and in the Talmud, and it explains why most of the haggadot concentrate on the socio-economic wickedness of the Sodomites.

The motif of haughtiness is again found with reference to the attitude of the Sodomites. They developed hubris because of the goodness of God. This is inferred from Job 28:5-8 which speaks of bread from the earth (the motif of fecundity), the earth being burned underneath (seen as the fire motif), and the richness of the earth in sapphires and gold dust (the motif of wealth). All of these are well-known in the Sodom and Gomorrah traditions. According to our text, wealth led to selfishness and emanated in xenophobia (the same sequence is found in Josephus, Ant 1:194; cf above, p 100). So they forbade travelling in their land in accordance with Job 28:4 which speaks of *hanniškâ ḥîm minnî râgèl*, 'those who are forgotten of foot'. In parallel versions the reference to Job 28:4 is meant as judgement over Sodom: God will cause them to be forgotten and a stream (i e of fire) will come over them (cf TSota 3:11-12, MekEx 15:1). Another parallel (WayyR 4:1) combines the xenophobia of the Sodomites with the motifs of hubris, wealth and injustice by using the Sodomites as an example of the meaning of Ecclesiastes 3:16 ('wickedness was in the place of justice'; cf also Midr Qoh 2:2). The same tradition is preserved a third time in the Midrash Rabbah (if we count BerR as well). This time (BemR 9:24) the Job text is combined with the clear-cut reference in Ezekiel 16:48-49 to the wealth as well as the socio-economic complacency of the Sodomites, and God says that he will sweep them away as they want to sweep away the 'alien foot' (i e, travellers) from their territory. The biblical emphasis on the social aspect of their wickedness, stemming as it does from the important function of the motif of hospitality in both the first and the second halves of the Sodom Cycle, is continually and thoroughly exploited by the Rabbinic use of the Sodom and Gomorrah tradition.

Returning to our text in Sanhedrin 109a-b, we find several haggadot expounding the cruelty and perverted sense of justice that obtained in Sodom, but also telling how the Sodomites could, on occasion, be outsmarted.

1. If a person was so poor that he had only one ox, he had to tend all the oxen of Sodom for one day; if he had no oxen, he had to toil even harder and tend them for two days. This absurd perversion of justice was unmasked by an orphan (one who is socially very weak) who killed all the oxen while on duty and helped himself to two rather than one hide on the basis of the principle that the end (consequence) of the law must match its beginning: no oxen - two days, no oxen - two hides.

2. The Sodomites would make their wickedness appear trivial by all openly stealing one brick or one onion at a time from one owner and so robbing him of his property by their combined effect. This represents the principle of creeping injustice which seems too small to punish, but which amounts to great wickedness.

3. The four judges of Sodom with their crooked names (cf above, p 108) also appear in this text. Their judgements are the opposite of justice. They would rule in favour of a man who assaults his neighbour's

wife and turn her over to the assailant who may make her pregnant 'for' her husband. Here the sexual motif clearly occurs in the service of the social motif. Basically it is what happens in the Sodom Cycle itself: The Sodomites are sinners in sexual respect, but this is a manifestation of their social wickedness.

4. They would pervert justice in favour of one who maims another's donkey.

5. They would make a complainant pay his assailant a 'bleeding' fee instead of making the aggressor pay damages.

6. A person who crosses into their territory by ferry had to pay one *zûz*, and whoever crossed the water on his own had to pay two *zûzîm* (later in the text the fees are respectively four and eight *zûzîm*, but the principle of double fees for less trouble given to the Sodomites, i e of the perversion of justice into its opposite, remains the same). A man who protested at this injustice was assaulted, literally experiencing injury added to injustice, and was made to pay his injurers for the injury: Injustice - injury - injustice.

7. Abraham's slave, Eliezer, suffered the same injustice, but himself wounded the judge in order to be paid the 'bleeding' money due to his own attacker. This again serves to demonstrate the palpable injustice which defeats itself.

8. Eliezer also outwitted the Sodomites when they required him to lie on their notorious bed. If a visitor was too tall for the bed, they would 'cut off some part of him (*gâyᵉzê minneh*)'; if he was too short, they would 'stretch him'. On the grounds of an oath sworn by him never to sleep on a bed, Eliezer refused to lie down. This shows how he saw through their wickedness.

9. Strangers would be given a *dinar* bearing the name of the donor, but no food. When the stranger died, each would come and take his money back. Why bother to give the money if they intend to get it back? – This is only understandable as a way of depicting the mockery made of social justice by tokenism. The same happens in the cases cited above where an assailant may make a woman pregnant as if doing her husband a favour (no 3) and where 'bleeding' money is mentioned (no 5).

10. No Sodomite was allowed to invite strangers to a feast. When Eliezer came there, he entered of his own accord and continually claimed to have been invited by the man sitting next to him, until all had fled for fear of being prosecuted. This haggadah not only shows that Eliezer was more resourceful than the Sodomites, but also depicts the cruel people as cowards and thereby testifies to an insight in the psychological make-up of the social bully.

11. The last of the string of haggadot in our text is the story of the girl

114

who dared to feed a poor man (in the parallel of BerR 49:6 she feeds a poor girl; cf p 107). According to this version of the story, she was daubed with honey and made to stand on a wall until the bees came and consumed her. Here the link between *rabbâ* in Genesis 18:20 and *rîbâ* ('girl'; Aramaic text: *ribtâ* = *riby^etâ*, *r^ebîtâ* = Hebrew *rîbâ*) is attributed to Rab (†247 CE; Bacher [1913] 1967:1-33) by his pupil Rabbi Jehudah ben Yechezkel (mid-third century CE; Bacher [1913] 1967:47-52). Here the girl's name is not given, but she is called Peletit in the Targumic version of the haggadah (TgJ1 on Gn 18:20-21) and in Pirqe deRabbi Eliezer. In the Targum Pseudo-Jonathan the penalty of death by burning for anyone who feeds strangers is built into the midrashic rendering of Genesis 18:20, and the cry of the maiden Peletit is mentioned in verse 21. The same story is also told in Pirqe deRabbi Eliezer 25. Here we have elements of both the earlier versions, pointing to a conflation of the various forms: Like in Sanhedrin 109b (and the Targum Pseudo-Jonathan), she feeds a poor man (*'anyâ*, not another girl) but, as in the version found in the Midrash Rabbah, she is burned to death, not devoured by bees. In all of these cases the extreme cruelty of the anti-social attitude of the Sodomites is illustrated. It is difficult to determine the origin of this haggadah. Mulder (1970:1-38) thinks that it probably originated in the school of Rabbi Aqiba in order to explain Genesis 18:20-21. It is possible, but the earliest literary manifestations of the story in Sanhedrin 109b and Bereshit Rabbah refer us to rabbis of the middle of the third and the beginning of the fourth centuries respectively. The story is obviously linked to Genesis 18:20-21, but it is not helpful in *explaining* the difficulty here, viz the implication that God did not know what was going on. In fact, it contributes nothing to this end. Verse 21 would still imply that God needed to come and learn facts that he did not know and in spite of the story we would still be where we were. I would rather say that the haggadah looks in quite another direction and that it *seizes upon* the text in Genesis 18:20-21 in order to give its own thrust a biblical foothold. This thrust is to illustrate that the 'great' (*rabbâ*) evil of Sodom is social cruelty.

Our witnesses point to the conclusion that the typical Rabbinic form of the Sodom and Gomorrah traditions was already shaped in the second century CE, and that this remained essentially the same in the third and fourth centuries. The typical Rabbinic form of the tradition entails its expression in the genre of haggadah in which the values of Rabbinic Judaism are expounded in narratives based on biblical texts. The Scriptures, forming as they do for the rabbis a unitary network of related references, may therefore be brought to bear on one another in order to articulate the beliefs of what had become mainstream Judaism. In this way the Sodom and Gomorrah traditions are compared to and interpreted in conjunction with several other words of Scripture. As to content, we may sum up our findings about the major motifs and their function as follows:

1. In Rabbinic circles the wickedness of the Sodomites was proverbial in a formal sense at least since the second century CE.

2. Rabbi Jehudah's idea of 'bodily' sin, the sexual aspect, is well attested.

3. It is, however, mostly subsumed under his idea of the Sodomite 'sin with money' and 'with bloodshed', i e the socio-economic aspect of the wickedness of Sodom is predominant in the Rabbinic texts.

4. The social aspect is developed by the logic: wealth - parsimony - social oppression.

5. Rabbi Jehudah finds this blasphemous at the same time because it is ultimately directed against God.

6. The fact that David is 'found' in Sodom, that Abram makes proselytes out of Sodomites, and that Lot's union with his daughters can become a pointer to the Messiah, shows that good can come from bad.

7. Lot is usually seen in an unfavourable light, but a good word can, on occasion, be found for him.

8. Angels are seen as superhuman creatures and a docetic interpretation of their appearance may be used to remain true to this belief.

4.6. Conclusions

If we take a bird's eye view of what we have found in the five paragraphs of this chapter, we see again that it is not possible to isolate a specific circle in which the Sodom and Gomorrah tradition/traditions were preserved and used. The fundamental motifs of the whole complex occur in the apocryphal and pseudepigraphical texts of the second and first centuries, in the works of historians and philosophers around the beginning of our era, and in the current which developed from the Pharisaic movement, right through to the fourth century CE. It is used in texts with a sapiential orientation (Ben Sira and the Wisdom of Solomon), in higher social circles (Ben Sira), in circles with an Essene religious background (the Testament of Abraham [?], Jubilees, the Apocalypse of Ezra), in Jewish philosophy indebted to Greek philosophy (Philo) and under the impact of Hellenistic society (Josephus), but it also occurs in the company of xenophobia (3 Maccabees).

Time and again the same basic motifs are found, viz wickedness and punishment, but the emphases and purposes which are served by them differ. Often the wickedness is of a generic nature (e g in the Apocrypha and Pseudepigrapha), but it is also often specified: The sexual motif is emphasised in the Testaments and Jubilees, but while it is given prominence in Rabbinic literature, it is subsumed under the social aspect, which is the most prominent in this corpus of literature. However, this aspect is also found in the works of Josephus and represents a development from the prophetic use of the Sodom motifs, which in turn is basically the same as that of the Sodom Cycle itself. Philo's use of the 'bodily' aspect of the Sodom motif is not only meant sexually, since in his system the passions of the body go further than this and include what we would call the economic aspect.

The punishment idea is developed into an eschatological symbol in the sapiential use of the tradition (Sap Sal) and in Jubilees, while the Mishnah also uses the Sodom tradition in this sense (Sanh 10:3). The wickedness-punishment theme is the most universal where the Sodom and Gomorrah tradition is used, but it is not the only way in which the tradition can function. It can be used to extol hospitality (TAbr – apart from the many places where this idea occurs alongside the more common theme of Sodom's punishment), and it can be used in a fossilised way to individuals (ApEzr), while the rabbis also testify to its use in a stereotyped form. The punishment theme matches Josephus's philosophy of history, while for Philo it expresses the demise of what is bodily as opposed to spiritual, and the whole tradition is used by him to exemplify his concept of God.

In view of this widely variegated use to which the same tradition is put, we must conclude to its being general property – from the time before the monarchy was instituted in Israel to the fourth century CE. The only period in which the preservation of the tradition cannot be followed clearly is, as far as I can see, between the fifth and the third centuries BCE.

5. Sodom and Gomorrah in early Christian literature

In this chapter the Sodom and Gomorrah traditions in both the New Testament and the early Fathers will be discussed as envisaged in the Introduction. For the former completeness can be claimed as far as the occurrence of the tradition is concerned. For the latter, however, the same goes as for the Rabbinic literature: I will endeavour to be representative, but completeness is, in the light of the vastness of the literature and the constraints of a study of this kind, at most a consummation devoutly to be wished but not to be attained.

5.1. The New Testament

The Sodom and Gomorrah tradition occurs in eight New Testament passages (nine if Mk 6:11 is also counted, which, in the light of the textual evidence, should probably not be done). In the following pages I shall endeavour to show that the use to which the tradition is put, is closely linked to the use made of it in the Jewish material that we have been studying, especially to a specific part of it, but that there is at the same time a certain narrowing down of the theme so that it is concentrated on one idea.

In **Matthew 10:15** we have a declaration that Sodom and Gomorrah will be better off in the day of judgement (*en hèmera kriseós*) than any city that refuses to receive the apostles or to listen to them. This immediately provides the basic traditional motifs present in the passage: The context is one of messengers being sent to cities, being received in the houses of some people and refused in other cases. The parallel to Genesis 19 is obvious: God's messengers were not treated with the necessary hospitality and the city was destroyed (cf Gnilka). The fact that the messengers of Genesis 19 were sent explicitly to destroy while those of Matthew 10 were sent to preach, is immaterial to the use of the Sodom example. Refusing to receive the messengers of the gospel is not only tantamount to the sin of the Sodomites, but worse. It is concluded *a minori ad maiorem* that the punishment on the day of judgment will be worse for such a city. Therefore it can be concluded that refusal to receive the messengers of the gospel is worse than the treatment given to God's messengers by the classic

118

symbols of depravity. The punishment to be meted out to such a city will take place on the day of judgement. This means that the Sodom and Gomorrah tradition here functions in an eschatological context. The same happens in **Luke 10:12** and (if we incorporate it in our list) **Mark 6:11.** The motifs of messengers (the number differs in the various texts), hospitality, rejection, punishment on the day of judgement (*hè hèmera ekeinè* in Lk 10:12) and comparison to Sodom and Gomorrah (only the Sodomites in Lk 10:12) are all present in these passages. We have further evidence in the New Testament that the motif of hospitality was expressed in terms of the Sodom story. Another element of tradition is the implication that the Sodomites will be present at the eschatological judgement. This was debated by the rabbis. Some rabbis thought that the Sodomites will not appear at the final judgement, which probably implies that they are already in everlasting damnation by virtue of the fire that rained down on them (cf Lang 1959:937-938; in Jude 7 this also seems to be the case). According to others the final punishment of the Sodomites is still to come (cf Sanh 10:3). Our three synoptic passages subscribe to the latter view. Nevertheless, if the burning of Sodom is to be 'reenacted in the eschaton' (Fitzmyer), its fate would not be as bad as that of the cities who have rejected the message of Jesus. Another implication in this use of the Sodom and Gomorrah tradition should not be overlooked. The two cities are taken as the norm of wickedness. If others are explicitly (as in Ezk 16:48) or implicitly (as in Mt 10 and Lk 10) said to be worse, it still means that the classic examples of wickedness remain the standard. The focus in these passages is, however, not on their wickedness, but on the final judgement. This means that our passages stand in the same current as some of the pseudepigrapha (Jub 16:5-9, 36:10; cf Lang 1959:937 for examples of fire as eschatological punishment in this literature).

The Gospel of Luke contains another passage in which the messengers of Jesus, a town, the inhospitality of its people and the motif of fire from heaven as punishment occur together: **Luke 9:51-56.** The motifs parallel to those in the passages that we have been considering are obvious, but there are also differences. The disciples, according to some manuscripts, compare the calling down of fire on the Samaritan town with what Elijah had done by calling down fire on the messengers of King Ahaziah (2 Ki 1:10.12). The Old Testament passage referred to does not speak of a city being burned, but of messengers who themselves meet this fate; neither is the fire a divine punishment for the sins of the people devoured by it. Even if the evidence for omission of the reference to Elijah (v 54, end) is strong (Marshall), it remains improbable that we here have a reference to the Sodom and Gomorrah tradition. The first reason for this is that Jesus is refused hospitality by the Samaritans not because they are opposed to his message, but because he is *en route* to Jerusalem, which would apply to any Jew passing through a Samaritan town. Second, Jesus rejects the idea of punishing the town with fire, stressing his mission to save rather than to destroy. Third, the idea of eschatological punishment is not present here at all, for the disciples want to see an immediate destruction of the town. These motifs are at variance with the explicit Sodom and Gomorrah passages in the Synoptics, where eschatological punishment for cities who reject the gospel is foreseen by Jesus himself.

In **Hebrews 13:2** a short injunction is found reminding the readers to remember hospitality. It is substantiated by the idea that hospitable people have been known to entertain angels without realising it. This is an obvious reference to Abraham and Lot in Genesis 18-19. It shows that the motif of hospitality as an element of the Sodom and Gomorrah tradition was not unknown in early Christianity, for the reference is cryptic and supposes that the readers would understand it.

Sodom without Gomorrah occurs in **Matthew 11:23.24.** According to Gnilka, Gomorrah is lacking because of the need to counterpoise the single city Capernaum to one other city. This is probably right, since in verses 21-22 two other Jewish cities, Chorazin and Bethsaida, are counterpoised to two other symbols of wickedness, Tyre and Sidon. There is a clear parallelism between the latter two on one hand and the former on the other. Again a Jewish city is unfavourably compared to Sodom. If Sodom had seen the miracles performed in Capernaum, it would not have been destroyed, but it would have remained until 'today' (*mechri tès sèmeron*). This not only makes the past topical for a later time (Gnilka), but it also shows that the insensitivity of Capernaum for the works of the Kingdom is worse than all the depravity of Sodom. Repentance wipes out all wickedness (cf the repentance motif in the parallel of v 21), but if the message of Jesus is refused, this possibility is also forfeited. Basically this boils down to the same as what we have seen in the passages on the sending of the messengers: Rejecting the message of Jesus is worse than Sodom's wickedness. Again this is linked to the eschatological judgement where Sodom will be treated more leniently than Capernaum.

Now we come to our last Synoptic passage, viz **Luke 17:22-37** in which Sodom occurs together with Lot. According to Zmijewski (1972:454-455) the figure of Lot, which only occurs here in the Synoptics, is not traceable to Q, but part of Luke's own contribution. Two examples from the Old Testament are given to illustrate the situation obtaining in Jesus' time when his own people rejected him (Rengstorff) or 'pursued their earthly existence with nonchalance' (Fitzmyer). The examples of Noah and Lot, that is, of the generation of the flood and that of Sodom, also occur together in Jewish literature and in other early Christian literature (cf the references below, p 123; a detailed discussion is given by Lührmann 1969:75-83, according to whom the primary function of this combination is to focus on punishment, while the rescue of the pious is secondary; cf also Schlosser 1973:13-36). The people of Jesus' time also indulged in feasting, drinking, planting (v 28 – the motif of fecundity in the Sodom tradition) and building. This is linked to their rejection of Jesus (v 25). If he is not accepted, the judgement will take place on the day of the revelation of the Son of Man (Zmijewski 1972:442; Schlosser 1973:35-36). Lot's wife (v 32) becomes a warning for the second and third generation Christians not to look back to what they have left behind when they have to flee Jerusalem (Rengstorff). The eschatological reference, however, has a direct bearing on the present, as Zmijewski (1972:487) rightly states. This represents the *function* of the Sodom and Gomorrah tradition in Luke 17: The Christians are to remember *now* what happened to Lot's wife, that is, their present life is to be influenced by what the Sodom and Gomorrah tradition teaches them as well as by the expectation of the coming day of the revelation of the Son of Man. Therefore the passage also has a positive aspect in that it calls to the acceptance of Jesus and to look forward expectantly. Sodom becomes a double symbol: Those who reject Jesus will be destroyed on the day of his revelation, and those who have accepted him but who have looked back to the past, will also be consumed.

Although Luke in general preserves the tradition of the earlier Christian generations so that his eschatology stands in continuity with the eschatology of this tradition (Zmijewski 1972:565-567), it is not so easy to establish whether the Sodom tradition in Luke 17 has been derived from Q (so Schnackenburg 1970:223) or added by Luke (so Zmijewski 1972:452-457). In my opinion such a nuanced debate is neither necessary nor helpful for an investigation such as the present one. We have established that the Sodom and Gomorrah tradition as reflected in the first century synoptic tradition (not only in Lk 17) was known and distinctively used by the early Christian community. That means that we may accept its presence in the second and third, and probably also in the first generations of the Christian tradition.

Sodom and Gomorrah occur once in the Pauline corpus of the New Testament. In **Romans 9:29** we encounter a quotation of Isaiah 1:9 as it appears in the Septuagint. Not so much the Sodom and Gomorrah of

Genesis as the use made of the theme in the Book of Isaiah is important in this text. The Hebrew text is about a 'remnant' (śārîd) that has been left in Israel, but for which Israel would have become like Sodom and Gomorrah, that is, completely exterminated (cf above, p 59). The Old Testament passage focusses on a punishment meted out to Israel from which only a remnant survived. Paul, however, focusses, not on the punishment, but on the remnant of Israel that has been spared in his own time. This is one reason why we may concur with Michel that the quotation from Scripture has a 'stronger' function than the thesis for which it is employed. Michel's own view is that Paul's argument develops the idea that God calls both Israel and the nations, while the quotation develops the idea that Israel was decimated while the nations were called to become part of God's people. This is important for Michel, since it suggests that the two quotations from Isaiah (Is 10:22 in v 27 and 1:9 in v 29) were already combined as Scriptural proof texts before Paul used them in the present context. This, in turn, would mean that the majority of Israel are condemned to destruction (Schmidt), and that the remnant represented by the first person plural of the quotation is the community of Jewish Christians who make up what is left of the true Israel (Wilckens). The Sodom and Gomorrah tradition again functions in an eschatological context since the whole argument of Paul is about the final salvation of Israel. In principle the Jewish Christians are like the remnant saved from the Isaianic 'Sodom' and in principle the majority of Jews are like the mass of Israel who did not survive the catastrophe of the Isaianic 'Sodom'. That is, the Jews will be surrendered to destruction in the final, eschatological judgement (cf Michel on vv 27.28). This painful situation is then considered by Paul from a new angle (Schmidt) and is, as a consequence, stood on its head when he reaches the conclusion with the help of another quotation from the Book of Isaiah (Is 59:20-21) that the whole Israel will after all be saved (Rm 11:26).

Two related passages containing the Sodom and Gomorrah tradition as we have seen it in i a the Pseudepigrapha are **Jude 7** and **2 Peter 2:6** (respectively the turn of the first/second century and some decades later). In fact, they are so closely related that the later of the two, can be regarded as dependent on the earlier (Bauckham, following the usual opinion in this matter; however, Schlosser 1973:31 points to the possibility that the two texts use a common source). In both cases (Jude 3-16, 2 Pt 2:1-22) the context speaks about false teachers. Moreover, in both texts outrageous sexual lust is a major issue, in both it is related to the Watchers and to the Sodomites, in both another traditional group of associates of the Sodomites occurs (the generation of the flood in 2 Pt and the generation of the wilderness in Jude). We have found these associations in several Jewish texts (Sir 16:7-10, 3 Macc 2:4, TNaph 3:4, Jub 16:5-9, Sanh 3:10, Sanh 110b; cf pp 76, 80, 81, and 125 on CD 2:16 - 3:12).

The sinful angels, the generation of the flood and the people of Sodom and Gomorrah (2 Pt 2:4.5.6 – mentioned in chronological order, cf Grundmann) are regarded as examples for what the false teachers do and what they can expect. The Watchers and the men of Sodom are the outstanding traditional examples of sexual aberrations, and this is also what the false teachers of early Christianity are accused of here (*epithymia*, 2 Pt 2:11). Accordingly they are to be punished on the eschatological 'day of judgement' (*hèmera kriseós*, 2 Pt 2:9). So we again have an application of what has happened in the past to what will happen in the future (Spicq). In the case of Sodom and Gomorrah it is explicitly said that they serve as an example or type (*hypodeigma*, 2 Pt 2:6) for the future. This means that Spicq is right when he takes the reference to the cities as a reference to 'le type par excellence des interventions punitives de Dieu' which speaks to the present about the past with a view to the future. The fact that Lot is saved is interpreted to the effect that he must have been a good man (*dikaios*, 2 Pt 2:7). This is balanced by the similar situation in the parallel example, where Noah (the preacher of *dikaiosynè*, 2 Pt 2:5) is saved. Our text thus aligns itself with that strand of the tradition in which Lot is not regarded as wicked, but as the opposite (cf above, pp 78, 83, 102; Sap 10:6, Jub 16:8-9; Ginzberg 1925:240, n 171 for references to the opposing traditions). In fact, Lot receives quite a moral testimonial (2 Pt 2:8).

Jude 7 also contains an instance of eschatological judgement (*puros aióniou dikè*). This fact, as well as the explicit reference to the Sodom and Gomorrah theme as a *deigma* (Jude 7, cf *hypodeigma* in 2 Pt 2:6) can be added to the list of similarities between the two passages given above. He also uses three examples (a fixed traditional phenomenon; cf Grundmann for further illustrations) of which Sodom is the third, but they are not in chronological order as in 2 Peter 2:4-6. Another difference between the two texts is that Jude mentions the other cities of the Pentapolis together with Sodom and Gomorrah, while 2 Peter only refers to the two most prominent cities of the group of five. It is obvious that we have here a schema which was traditionally established and used in the early church. The sexual motif is abundantly clear in this passage. The Watchers were angels who united sexually with human women (cf Gn 6:1ff) and the lust of the men of Sodom was likewise after angels (Gn 19:4ff). Therefore something of the same nature must be intended in the case of the false teachers, since it is said explicitly that they 'practiced sexual immorality in the same way as they', i e the angels (*ton homoion tropon toutois ek-*

porneusasai) and that they also 'went after strange flesh' (*apelthousai opisó sarkos heteras*). The moot point is what exactly this refers to. According to Bauckham it is not homosexual practice since 'strange flesh' cannot refer to this but only to the flesh of the angels. However, he adds that 'we can hardly speculate that they desired sexual relations with the angels – even in their "dreams" (v 8)'. He thinks that, instead, the false teachers rebelled 'against the divinely established order of things' and that , 'in doing so they were motivated, like the Watchers and Sodomites, by sexual lust'. What would this be if not either homosexual practice or perverse lust for angelic flesh or, perhaps, a combination of the two in which the lust for angels is enacted homosexually? This is not the most convincing of Bauckham's arguments, since *ton homoion tropon* must mean that they indeed desired sex with either men or with angels. In any case the sin of Sodom is here seen as a sexual aberration for which the punishment is everlasting hellfire.

Excursus: Sodom and Gomorrah in Qumran and the Samaritan community

At this juncture we may notice the absence of any appreciable development of the Sodom and Gomorrah traditions in Qumran as opposed to Samaritan literature. Strictly speaking, these observations have their place in the chapter on early Jewish literature, but they are better made after the treatment of the tradition in 2 Peter and Jude (cf the interesting reference by Bauckham to the Damascus Document in the course of his comments on Jude 5-7). As far as I can see, it only occurs in the biblical manuscripts and the retelling of Genesis 13-14 in the Genesis Apocryphon. It is not exploited as in the rest of contemporary Jewish literature, while one would have expected the Qumran community to welcome the biblical symbol of a wicked city which could be applied to Jerusalem (as was done in Christianity, cf Rv 11:8). In contemporary writings, as we have seen repeatedly (cf the references above, p 123), Sodom is found in the company of the Watchers/giants, the generation of the flood, the generation of the dispersion, the generation of the wilderness, and the Egyptians (cf Bauckham's list, which is heavily influenced by Schlosser 1973:25-35). This can be extended still by a number of cases in the Samaritan Memar Marqah (about the third or even the fourth century CE). Here Sodom, Sodom and Gomorrah, and the Sodomites often occur in short references. In several of these instances we find the Sodomites in the company of members of Schlosser's schema (e g the generation of the flood, the generation of the dispersion, the generation of the wilderness, Egypt), and often the list is augmented by comparable figures (e g Cain,

Enosh, Cush, Nimrod, Lamech, Amalek, Babel, Korah). In fact, this schema is a dominant feature of the Memar Marqah (cf 1:1.3, 2:4, 3:5.7, 4:4.5.9.10.12, 6:2 – sometimes more than once in a paragraph). Now it is noteworthy that the same context, or 'schéma traditionnel', as Schlosser calls it, is found in the Damascus Document (CD 2:16 - 3:12). However, no mention of Sodom is made here. In fact, this is the only instance known to me where Sodom, one of its core examples (Bauckham), is lacking from the schema. We clearly have a traditional list which was used for centuries (at least from before Ben Sira, i.e. the third century BCE, to the time of the Memar Marqah, i.e. the third or fourth century CE; cf Macdonald 1963:xx). So it is natural to expect the presence of Sodom as one of its dominant motifs where this schema is used.

The same goes for the Genesis Apocryphon. Here Sodom is mentioned only to identify the place where Lot went to live and to identify the king who was rescued by Abram (1QapGn 21:6, 22:1.12.18.20.25). The biblical narrative of Genesis 13 and 14 is retold. However, the sins and the ruin of Sodom are not introduced where it is most expected (1QapGn 21, where the parallel to the passage containing Gn 13:13 is found). This is even more remarkable than it would have been if the word $s^e dom$ were lacking altogether. Why would an opportunity to criticise the traditional symbol of evil be avoided so obviously (cf Schlosser 1971:22, who finds the silence in this document remarkable and serious)?

There must be a reason for its absence from the Damascus Document and in the Genesis Apocryphon as well as for the lack of interest in Sodom elsewhere in the Qumran writings. Could it be that the site of Qumran, near the Dead Sea (albeit its north-western side) with its reminiscences of Sodom and the rest of the Pentapolis, made these cities less than attractive as symbols of wickedness to the people of Qumran? After all, the cities are a *deigma* of wickedness and punishment (cf Jude 7, 2 Pt 2:6, 3 Macc 2:5) which can still be recognised in the permanently devastated landscape of the region (cf Josephus, BJ 4:485; also Lang 1959:945-946 and above, pp 97-98). And this is the vicinity where the fallen angels, so often associated with Sodom, are imprisoned – almost as the fellow inmates of the people of Qumran!

On the other hand it is remarkable that the Sodom and Gomorrah tradition appears so often in the Memar Marqah. This is an important text of the Samaritan community and as such makes comparison with the Qumran community possible. Notwithstanding the difference in date, we have two well-defined and isolated religious communities within the parameters of early Judaism. The literature of the one community is very sparse with regard to the Sodom tradition and the other is obvious for its copious reference to the tradition. The Memar Marqah often contains the schema pointed out by Schlosser (cf above), but it also exploits other aspects of the Sodom and Gomorrah tradition. This is done in short references to the angels of Genesis 18 and 19 (e.g. 1:1; in 1:3 they are seen as types of Moses and Aaron), or in a comparison of Mount Gerizim to Sodom, its opposite (3:5), the 'deed' of the Sodomites in a rejection of sexual perversity (3:7, 4:5), the 'deed' of Lot in another sexual reference (3:5), Sodom and Gomorrah as evil places (4:10, with reference to Dt 32:22, cf 4:5 where this text is also referred to), God as the one who turned over Sodom (*'šlyt sdm*) as opposed to Eden (4:12), and Abram's shield in Sodom (4:12, with reference to Gn 14:22), and the folly of the Sodomites (6:2; cf Sap 10:6-9). This throws into relief the practical absence of interest in Sodom among the people of Qumran.

Our last New Testament reference to Sodom is **Revelation 11:8** (end of the first century CE). Here Sodom is only a figurative or 'spiritual' name for Jerusalem (cf *pneumatikós*), the city 'where our Lord was crucified'. It functions as a derogatory name since Sodom is the most sinful city of all. There are, of course, antecedents for calling Jerusalem by this name (Is 1:9.10; cf Jr 23:14, Ezk 16:48). In our text we hear of a catastrophe, but Sodom is not used as the symbol of the final judgement. Neither is there any mention of fire and brimstone, which does occur several times elsewhere in the Book of Revelations (Rv 9:17.18, 14:10, 19:20, 20:10, 21:8). This mostly refers to the woes of hell and may be influenced by the motif of punishment by fire and brimstone in Genesis 19:24 as well as the idea that the fallen angels were imprisoned beneath the Dead Sea (1 Enoch 67:4-13, Origen, Cels 5:52). Lang (1959:946) finds that the motif of Sodom's punishment and the geographical condition of the Dead Sea region 'clearly' influenced the idea of a 'sea of fire' found in the Book of Revelations. It is entirely possible, but I would prefer to be less emphatic in such claims.

In sum, we may say the following about the Sodom and Gomorrah traditions in the New Testament:

1. Sodom and Gomorrah remain the standard example of wickedness and God's punishment.

2. The tradition is always used in an eschatological context, sometimes with reference to the damnation of hell and sometimes in a broader sense.

3. In the Synoptics it is primarily used to underscore the expected punishment of those who refuse to accept the message of Jesus, which is several times expressed by means of the hospitality motif so entrenched in the oldest strata of the Sodom tradition.

4. In Luke the tradition is also used positively for the present life of Christians, encouraging them to look forward expectantly.

5. While Sodom is once used as a pejorative name for Jerusalem, the Jewish Christians are seen as the remnant who were spared the fate of the Isaianic 'Sodom'.

6. Only in the latest documents of the New Testament is the sexual motif of the Sodom and Gomorrah tradition emphasised.

In using the Sodom and Gomorrah traditions the New Testament concentrates on the meaning of Jesus' message and salvation. We may, therefore, conclude that the sexual aspect, while present, receives as little prominence in the New Testament as it does in the Old and in the early Jewish literature. What has happened that the word 'sodomy' in later parlance came to mean 'perverse sexuality' or 'homosexual practice'? Perhaps we shall find a clue to the answer in the last paragraph of our study.

5.2. Patristic literature

This section has to cover the most diverse authors and their use of the Sodom and Gomorrah tradition. Again I will content myself with an endeavour at being representative. We shall follow the same *modus operandi* as in the other chapters by working through the texts where the Sodom and Gomorrah tradition is found. The texts are discussed in chronological order instead of, as one often finds, in two rather artificial groups called the 'Greek Fathers' and the 'Latin Fathers' (cf the references that we have already encountered in some Syrian Fathers).

The earliest Father who refers to Sodom, is **Clement of Rome**, one of the Apostolic Fathers, whose **Letter to the Corinthians** contains two references to our tradition (1 Clem 10:4, 11:1-2). In the first of these mention is made of the separation of Abraham and Lot (Gn 13), but not of the city of Sodom itself. In the second Lot's rescue is ascribed to his hospitality (*philoxenia*) and piety (*eusebeia*). He was one of those who have hope (*elpizein*) in God. Those who turn to others are punished and tormented. This implies that the Sodomites had turned to other (gods) and were destroyed for this reason. The Sodom tradition therefore functions here as part of a polemic against pagan gods (cf Tertullian, Ap 50:7, where the same function of the tradition occurs). It is possible that Clement's use of *philoxenia* here alludes to Hebrews 13:2, since it is a favourite word of his (also found, with its cognates, in 1 Cl 1:2, 10:7, 12:1.3, 35:5; cf Hagner 1973:193, who points out 'Clement's pleasure in identifying personages alluded to but unnamed by the writer to the Hebrews'). Lührmann (1972:130) thinks that we here find an instance of the combination of the motifs of the flood and of Sodom which we have often encountered in the Apocrypha, Pseudepigrapha, Rabbinic literature and the New Testament (cf also Schlosser 1973:25). I doubt this, however, since Noah and the flood are only mentioned two chapters earlier (1 Clem 9:4) and there is no direct link between the references. The occurrence of both the flood and Sodom should rather be ascribed to the nature of the argument being developed (Old Testament examples are advanced in support of the Christian message) than to a received Jewish tradition (cf Hagner 1973:247). Why would its elements be separated and used apart from each other? In the same passage Lot's wife is used as a warning for all generations not to look back to the life that lies behind. This refers to Christians who have broken with the past, that is, with the life of 'turning to other gods'. Christians should not long for the pre-Christian, Sodom-type of life.

The Sodom theme occurs three times in the **Dialogue with Trypho** by **Justin Martyr**, one of the Greek apologists of the second century. All of these are in the context of a defense of the Christian concept of God against that of a Jew. In the first case Tr 55) Isaiah 1:9 is used somewhat like the use made of it in Romans 9:29 (cf above, p 122): Justin tells Trypho that only a remnant of the Jews have not become like Sodom. The next case (Tr 56) is an extensive argument in defense of the conviction that Christ as God appeared to Abraham at Mambre. The argument is: God appeared to Abraham according to Genesis 18. However, God was in heaven and did not speak directly to humans. Then God who appeared to Abraham cannot be the same as God who was in heaven. So it must have been Christ, who is God and who appeared as a man on earth. The three visitors were, accordingly, Christ plus two angels. These two angels were sent to destroy Sodom. However, God himself addressed Lot in Sodom. This Lord, distinct from the Lord in heaven, was to destroy Sodom. In the whole argument specific use is made of Genesis 18:1-3 and 19:23-25. Without being too explicit, Justin exploits the singular/plural issue in the Sodom chapters in support of his view that God became a man and appeared as such to the patriarchs. The last case (Tr 128) serves the same purpose. Here Justin says that it was Christ who punished the Sodomites (cf Irenaeus, Epideixis 44, where the same motif is found). He defends the deity of Christ with the help of Old Testament texts.

Our next Church Father is one of the most important theologians of the second century, **Irenaeus of Lyon** (c 130-200). He also uses the Sodom tradition for the presentation of the Christian faith. In his argument against the heretics he takes recourse to the Sodom theme several times. First (**Adv Haer 4:36,3**) he makes it part of an admonition to be alert for no one knows when the Lord will come. With reference to Matthew

11:23.24, 24:42 and Luke 17:26ff he combines the motif of Noah and the flood with that of Sodom. This time it is done explicitly and we may register the text as another Christian occurrence of the traditional Jewish combination of the flood and Sodom. This also happens in the next paragraph (**Adv Haer 4:36,4**). Here the tradition of the Watchers is also mentioned; the angels mixed with humans and a sinful generation ensued. This confirms the presence of the old Jewish combination of traditions. Another interesting feature is that the union between the angels and the humans is regarded as the cause of an offspring who cannot be fruitful for God. This is ambiguous and can refer to their physical barrenness (which would fit the motif of barrenness so often found in the Sodom and Gomorrah traditions and used expressly for sexual barrenness by Philo, Abr 135) as well as to their moral inability to produce good deeds (which suits the accompanying reference to Lk 3:9 about unfruitful trees that will be destroyed by fire). One of the 'points more or less „peculiar"' (Smith 1952:42) in the theology of Irenaeus can be seen in this text. According to him the Word was responsible for the destruction of Sodom by fire and brimstone from heaven. He does not say that Christ did the punishing (as Justin, Tr 128, does), but he finds the punitive action of the Word an illustration of the fair judgement of God (2 Th 1:5). The Word did several 'peculiar' things (Smith), like being responsible for God's walking with the first humans in paradise and bringing about the theophanies of the Old Testament. Probably this serves to show that Christ communicates positively with humans as well as punitively. The call to alertness is enhanced by the use of the Sodom and Gomorrah tradition in the admonitory function given it by Matthew: It will be better for these two cities in the day of judgement than for those who reject the message of the apostles of Christ.

Irenaeus also uses the Sodom and Gomorrah tradition in his *Epideixis tou apostolikou kèrygmatos*, known in an Armenian translation since 1904. Here (**Epid 20**) he classifies the Sodomites with the Canaanites, Hittites, Amorites, Egyptians and others as nations who are subsumed under the curse of Canaan by Noah (Gn 9:25). The implication seems to be that they are all 'Canaanites'. Smith (1952:157 n 106) has noticed however, that this is, as far as the Sodomites are concerned, not in accordance with Genesis 10:19, where the boundary of Canaan is 'until you enter Sodom'. He does not pursue the matter, but the observation is right (cf my argument above, pp 49-50). Further on in the same work (**Epid 44**) Irenaeus exploits the double reference to God in Genesis 19:24 in support of the conviction that it was the Son of God who was given the authority by the Father to punish the Sodomites. Since God appeared to Abraham before that (Gn 18:1.2), it was the same Son who came to Abraham in the company of two angels. As we have seen Justin do, and as we shall see Tertullian do (cf below), the story of Sodom and Gomorrah is used as a proof text for the Christian concept of God.

Clement of Alexandria lived at the turn of the second to the third century (*c* 150-215). In his 'Exhortation' the Sodom theme occurs with a sharply negative tone but at the same time in the context of a call or 'exhortation' to turn to God **(Protr 10)**. Clement polemises against the idols who are made of dead stone and wood. Whoever prays to a dead stone becomes one himself. This is illustrated by the examples of Niobe and of Lot's wife. The latter became stone (*lelithomenè*) because she loved Sodom (cf Gn 19:26). It is therefore understandable that the vices of the Sodomites include insensibility (they were *èlithioi*), a word which calls to mind the word for 'stone' (*lithè*) and the verb just used. The sins of the Sodomites also include hardness of heart (they were *sklèrokardioi*), impiety (*asebeia*) and atheism (they were *atheoi*). All of this leads to the assurance that the way to God is open, and to the exhortation to come to the knowledge of God. The Sodom and Gomorrah tradition thus becomes a device for arguing against the idols, who are not really gods, and to convince people to turn to the true God lest they be punished by his wrath.

Many short references are made to the Sodom and Gomorrah tradition by the prolific Latin author of the third century, **Tertullian** († after 220), in works from both his Catholic and his Montanist periods. In his Apology, which hails from his Catholic period, about 197 CE, he answers the political accusation that the Christians unduly despise the gods of the State. For this purpose he combines the motifs of the flood and Sodom (**Ap 40:7, 26**), thereby continuing an old Jewish tradition. The gods must be later than the flood, or they would not have survived it. The Jews (*sic*) were not yet in Palestine when the rain of fire destroyed Sodom and Gomorrah, those *regiones adfines eius*, that is, those regions bordering on Palestine (cf my argument on p 49 and Smith 1952:157 n 106). In this context Tertullian also refers to the apples of Sodom that turn to dust as one touches them (cf his knowledge of the region, **Pall 2:4,44**) as well as to the smell of burning which was still hanging over the Sodom region in his day. Now Tuscany and Campania had not begun to complain against the Christians when they were hit by catastrophes, one of these being a fire from heaven (*de caelo...ignis*) which destroyed Volsinii, and Pompeii was destroyed by fire from its own mountain. This is an obvious parallel to Sodom. Since catastrophe befell the gods themselves, it proves both that they are incapable of saving their territory and that the Christians are not to blame on the grounds of their disdain for such gods. The Christians are as innocent of these catastrophes as the Jews are of the catastrophe of

Sodom. We here have an effective argument based on Christian conviction, knowledge of the Scriptures and history, as well as a sound juridical background.

Tertullian, like Justin and Irenaeus, made use of Genesis 19:24 to expound his concept of God. If the Lord made the fire and brimstone rain from the Lord, the fact that he is mentioned twice cannot be unimportant. There is only one God, so the text must, so to speak, have a christological meaning. That is, it must refer to the Father and to Christ (**Prax 13:247,21, 16:256,21**). Furthermore, Genesis 18:21 is as much a problem for Christians as for Jews. Does God have to come down to earth because he does not know what is going on in Sodom and Gomorrah? While the rabbis referred to the haggadah of the girl of Sodom (cf Sanh 109b and parallels), Tertullian claims that God descended not because he was ignorant, but because he does what he pleases and in this case it was his will to come down and see; therefore he uses the future tense *videbo*, showing that he *will* see if he pleases (**Adv Mar 2:25:371,20**). The angels who accompanied him were on earth in physical form (**Carn Chr 3:41**; cf Thunberg 1966:563-564), which is the opposite of what Philo believed (cf QuaestGn 4:9). This should not surprise us, since Tertullian was a stalwart opponent of Gnostic docetism. Against Marcion's claim that the Old Testament concept of God differs from that of the New, Tertullian employs the Sodom tradition: If the God of the New Testament can send fire (which Marcion does not deny), then the God of the Old Testament, who does the same according to the Sodom story, does not differ from him (**Adv Mar 4:29:523,4**).

The Sodom tradition as used in Isaiah 1:10 is also attested in the works of Tertullian. The leaders of Israel are called Sodomites. It is understandable that Tertullian would call the spiritual leaders of the established religious community 'Sodomites' in this period of his career. These references occur in texts hailing from his Montanist, anti-Catholic period (**Adv Mar 3:13:398,15, 4:27:514,15**, cf **Adv Iud 9:94**). He also uses the tradition as an injunction not to look back (cf Clement of Alexandria, Prot 10). Lot's wife is an example of the danger of harking back to what lies in the past (**Adv Mar 4:23:499,22**). In the light of the implication that the leaders of the established church are 'Sodomites', this probably refers to the Catholic past as opposed to the Montanist future rather than to the pre-Christian/Christian eras in an individual's life. Tertullian regarded Lot, in contradistinction to the latter's wife, as a meritorious person, thus aligning himself with another old Jewish tradition (**Adv Iud 2:90**, cf Ginzberg 1925:240, n 171). The same idea is suggested in a later pseudo-Tertullian text, **Sodoma** (Migne, PL 2,1101-1106). This is a poem which tells the story of Lot and the destruction of Sodom. It adds a number of embellishments, mostly containing motifs known from the Jewish tradition, especially in terms reminiscent of Josephus. Lot is presented as a wise colonist, the only one in Sodom to remember God (*Transvena Loth aderat, sapiens, justique colonus, /Unus erat, meminisse Deum*; cf Josephus, Ant 1:200-202a). The motif of the pulverising apples, used by Tertullian in the Apology (cf Josephus, BJ 4:484), appears in the third section of the poem. The desolate character of the Dead Sea vicinity is depicted in much the same way as in the Jewish descriptions we have encountered (cf Josephus, BJ 4:453). Even the tenacity of the bitumen found in the region is described in the same way as by Josephus (BJ 4:480). The well established combination of the flood and Sodom, which we have found in many Jewish texts, but also in the New Testament (cf above, pp 120-123), Irenaeus (Adv Haer 4:36,3) and Tertullian (Ap 40:7,26) is used in the opening section of the poem.

Finally, Tertullian employs the Sodom and Gomorrah tradition for the purposes of a typically Montanist warning against marriage. People marry daily, but, in pursuing the preoccupations of married life, they will be taken by surprise when the day of judgement arrives as suddenly as the day of destruction over Sodom and Gomorrah (**Cast 9:42**, cf **Mon 16:6,25**, **Ux 1:5:24**; the latter text is from the earlier Catholic period and the other two from the Montanist period – illustrating how Tertullian leaned in this direction before he became a Montanist). His Montanist insistence on *poenitentia* was also expressed by means of the Sodom tradition. Whereas Sodom and Gomorrah did not repent, it is possible to turn away from one's sins in which case God will not be angry as he was at the wicked cities (**Ie 7:282,20**).

One of the three 'great Cappadocians', **Basil the Great** (*c* 330-379), was known for his interest in practical matters of church life and his constructive activities on the orthodox side during the Arian controversies of the fourth century (cf Altaner & Stuiber 1966:290-291). Both of these facets of his career can be seen in a short reference to Sodom in his letter to orthodox monks who were harassed by Arians (**Letter 257**). The letter encourages the monks not to be daunted by the harassment. They can expect a reward for remaining steadfast. Neither the masses nor the Arian clergy should intimidate them and they should remember that Christ himself was prosecuted by priests. So, even if they are all overcome and only one is saved like Lot among the Sodomites, he should not doubt his *orthè krisis*, his right judgement, but remain orthodox. The fact that three people, not one, were saved according to the Sodom story, shows that Basil's reading of the Sodom story is coloured by his own situation in the Arian controversy. The Arian environment becomes a manifestation of

132

Sodom and the possibility of a solitary orthodox monk surrounded by 'Sodomites' becomes an illustration of a Lot-type salvation.

Another saint sometimes called 'the Great', **Macarius of Egypt** (c 300 - c 390) also illustrates how his own background determines his use of the Sodom and Gomorrah tradition. Macarius lived an ascetic life in the desert of Scetis and was the father of the most prominent centre of Egyptian monasticism. Contemporaries do not mention his literary activities (Altaner & Stuiber 1966:264), but several writings are attributed to him. Among these are the **Visions of sacred angels** (Sanc Ang). In the second part of this text (Migne PG 34,225 A) Macarius is said to have claimed that he saw the heavens open and angels move around. A human soul who had practised *porneia* was brought in to the *archón tou telóniou*, the head of the toll house (where the souls are stopped for examination). In answer to a question by the head the angels said that this soul had practiced sexual immorality all his life and had committed 'the Sodomite sin' many times. It is not clear whether 'the Sodomite sin' is seen as something different from ordinary *porneia* or as the same. In the former case the reference would probably be to homosexual practice. In any case, the sin of Sodom is here regarded as sexual offences, which fits the monastic ideals of Macarius.

Another ascetic of the fourth century, the Latin Father **Jerome** (c 347-420), likewise employed the Sodom and Gomorrah tradition in the service of his views on sexuality and marriage. His famous **Letter to Eustochium**, probably dating from 384 (Lawler & Mierow 1963:233), is addressed to Eustochium who was later to succeed her mother as head of the convent at Bethlehem. The letter strongly advocates virginity and self-restraint. Both themes are expressed with the help of the Sodom story (Ad Eust 2 and 8). First Eustochium is addressed as the bride of Christ and virginity is praised. While marriage is not wrong, it has many disadvantages (cf the views of Tertullian on this issue, Cast 9:42, Mon 16:6,25, Ux 1:5:24). When leaving Sodom, Eustochium is to remember the wife of Lot who looked back to the sinful city (cf Ad Rufin 4, where, according to Lawler & Mierow 1963:194, a cryptic reference to Lot's wife is present, but this is doubtful). Here the ideas of virginity and avoiding to revert to earlier life are combined (cf Clement of Alexandria, Prot 10, and Tertullian, Adv Mar 4:23:499,22). The other aspect of Jerome's asceticism is reflected further on (Ad Eust 8), where he warns against wine. The obvious examples are cited, viz Noah and Lot. Both are treated with some sympathy; Noah was probably unaware that wine would make him drunk, whereas the daughters of Lot did not pursue lust since they thought that the whole human race was eradicated. Lot himself was ignorant of what was going on, but even so both episodes go to show to what terrible results wine leads (it was the cause of the birth of Moab and Ammon, Israel's enemies). The combination of Noah and Lot in this letter is probably not influenced by the traditional combination of the flood and Sodom, since the two examples are germane to Jerome's cause in their own right: The first refers to the first drinking of wine on earth and the second also suggests the sexual motif.

In his **Commentary on Ezekiel 16** Jerome derides the Jews for thinking that Sodom is to be restored. Aphraates is also acquainted with this haggadah which is, however, only known from one Jewish source (Tanchuma Gn 47B; Ginzberg 1900:110).

Jerome translated and revised a geographical work by **Eusebius** (c 260-340), called *Peri tón topikón onomatón en tè theia graphè* (cf Klostermann 1966). It is worth mentioning since it contains references to Sodom and the other Pentapolis cities, giving geographical detail and such information as the different names of Zoar (*Bala, Sigór, Zoora*; Latin: *Bala, Segor, Zoara*).

As Tertullian answered the accusation that the Christians are to blame for the misfortunes of Rome in his Apology, so **Augustine** (354-430), with whom we shall end this study, defended Christianity against the resurgence of similar clamours after the fall of Rome to Alaric in 410. He did this in his main apologetic work, **De civitate Dei**, which was written between 413 and 426 (cf Altaner & Stuiber 1966:424). Sodom and Gomorrah are mentioned several times, especially in Book 16. All of these references are not equally important. However, some are significant not because they are original, but because they demonstrate that certain motifs from the Sodom and Gomorrah tradition, having been taken up by Augustine, became seminal in later usage due to the enormous influence of Augustine.

Our first passage (Civ 10:8) finds itself in the context of Augustine's proposition that the wonders of old strengthen faith in God. The Sodom Cycle is not devoid of evidence in this regard: Abraham and Sarah became parents in old age (Gn 21:2); fire devoured Sodom like it devoured Abraham's sacrifice (cf Gn 15:17); angels appeared to Abraham in the form of men (*angeli hominibus similes*); the same angels miraculously rescued Lot when the fire was already threatening. In addition, Lot's wife is a warning to those who have started off on the road of freedom (*via liberationis*) not to look back to the life behind them. Not only the latter motif (advanced by Clemens Alexandrinus, Tertullian and Jerome), but all of them have been received by Augustine from the Judeo-Christian tradition and are used in much the same way as by his Christian predecessors.

In Book 16 we find many references to material in the Sodom and Gomorrah tradition. Several of them are of minor importance as they serve to orientate the reader and to explain the family relations involved in Abraham's career. According to Augustine a new era begins with Abraham, and his relatives, including Lot, are mentioned (Civ 16:12.13). Lot's importance lies in the fact that he accompanied Abraham on the jopurney commanded him by God (Civ 16:15.18). Lot is even used by Augustine to cover up Abraham's lie about his relationship to Sarah (Gn 12:13); if Lot can be called Abraham's brother (Gn 13:8), then Sarah can be called his sister – so Abraham was not a liar (Civ 16:19). Augustine also refers to the separation between Abraham and Lot, after which Lot went to live *in Sodomis*, among the Sodomites (Gn 13; Civ 16:20.21), and to the narrative of Genesis 14, where Abraham came to the rescue of his kinsman and the Sodomites, refusing to take spoil from the king of Sodom (Civ 16:22). These details show that Augustine made thorough use of the Sodom and Gomorrah tradition and they prepare the ground for the theologically more important passages.

In **De civitate Dei 16:29** Augustine explores the trinitarian possibilities of Genesis 18-19. Whereas Justin, Irenaeus and Tertullian use the singular/plural issue in Genesis 18-19 in support of the idea that Christ must have been one of them, Augustine rejects it. His argument is that the oscillation of singular and plural is found in both halves of the story, in Genesis 18 as well as in Genesis 19. If Christ was one of the *three* angels who visited Abraham and was addressed as 'Lord' by Abraham, then why does Lot also address the *two* angels as 'Lord' when the Lord remained behind at Mamre to listen to Abraham's intercession for Sodom? Augustine sees the problem with the logic of the text, but his solution does not gain in clarity. He thinks that Abraham recognised the Lord in all three men and that Lot recognised the Lord in the two who came to him (*Abraham in tribus et Loth in duobus viris Dominum agnoscebat*). Therefore they used the singular even though the visitors were thought to be men (*etiam cum eos homines esse arbitrarentur*). If 'the Lord' (*Dominus*) was present, was Christ present? Augustine leaves the question unanswered. Thunberg (1966:563) attributes this to Augustine's idea of 'the limited character of the knowledge of God within the Old Covenant'. Theologically, Augustine cannot admit a revelation of Christ in human form prior to the incarnation. His handling of the matter rather resembles the ambivalence of the biblical text itself. It is not impossible that Augustine left the problem ambivalent intentionally? Whether so or not, he captured the spirit of the way in which the author of the Sodom Cycle referred to God.

The following chapter, **De Civitate Dei 16:30**, tells of the destruction of Sodom by 'a fiery storm from heaven' (*igneo imbre de caelo*). Lot's wife is again held up as a warning to Christians not to 'look back' (cf Civ 10:8), this time with the addition that her saltiness serves as seasoning for believers with the salt of wisdom not to follow her example. The only wickedness of the Sodomites mentioned, is that they practised homo-sexual deeds (*stupra in masculos*) which was practically sanctioned by law. This may reflect knowledge of the Jewish haggadah about the perverse judiciary in Sodom (cf Sanh 109a-b), but the noteworthy thing is that Augustine regards homosexuality as 'the Sodomite sin'. From this time on neither the social awareness of the Old Testament Sodom traditions nor that of the Jewish reception of these traditions is to be found in the centre of the Sodom and Gomorrah theme. A new motif has come to the fore, where it has stayed ever since – 'sodomy'.

Augustine also knows about the apples of Sodom (Civ 21:7), and he thinks the men of Sodom were not totally blind, or they would not have searched for Lot's door after having been blinded (Civ 22:19). A last minor reference to the Sodom tradition is contained in Augustine's con-viction that the punishment of Sodom and that of Nineveh illustrate two kinds of punishment by God: Either the sinners or the sins may be swept away, respectively when the sinners do not repent and when they do (Civ 21:24).

A note on the Christian interpretation of the angels in Genesis 18

We have found several interpretations of the Mamre scene as part of the use made by the early Fathers of the Sodom and Gomorrah traditions. There are also several patristic texts in which the authors do not focus on the Sodom tradition so much as on the theological problem of God's appearance to humans, in this case to Abraham. These have been collected and studied by Thunberg (1966:560-570). Thunberg's analysis can be squared with what we have seen in the exposition given above, although some of the authors treated by him fall outside the period to which we have limited ourselves. According to Thunberg the early Christian inter-pretations of the three angels can be divided into three groups.

The first is the literal interpretation where the visitors are seen as angels and no more. This is associated with the Antiochene tradition: Eutherius of Tyana (*c* 434; Conf 13); Theodoret of Cyrrhus (*c* 393 - *c* 466; Quaest in Gn 69); John Chrysostom (*c* 347 - *c* 407; Hom in Gn 18).

Secondly, there is the christological interpretation where one of the three visitors is seen as Christ: Novatian (third century; De Trin 18); Tertullian (cf above); Hilary of Poitiers (*c* 315-367; De Trin 4:27-29);

Justin Martyr (cf above). Here it should be added that Justin and Tertullian, like Irenaeus, also make use of Genesis 19:24 in support of their view and in so doing use the whole of the Sodom narrative for their purposes. Also Origen (*c* 185 - *c* 254) is classified under the christological interpreters. He provided a classic formulation, which is nevertheless unclear: *Tribus occurrit et unum adorat et ad unum loquitur* (In Gn Hom 4:2, Latin translation by Rufin). Christ was one of the three, but the Father was adored. Interpretations in this category are also found in the formulations of the Council of Sirmium (351), Pseudo-Chrysostom (Migne, PG 56, 546) and Cyril of Jerusalem (Migne, PG 33, 744A).

The last category is the trinitarian interpretation. Here we find emphasis on Abraham's knowledge of God and on the difference between the appearance to him and the appearance to Lot. Origen on occasion also seems to favour this interpretation (In Cant 2: *nam Trinitatis ibi mysterium prodebatur*). Others are Cyril of Alexandria († 444; Contr Jul 1), Tertullian who sometimes also interprets the passage in a trinitarian way (Spir Sanct 1, 6), and Augustine who sometimes reads the passage in this way as well (cf above and Contr Max, where he says that Abraham saw three men with his bodily eyes while the eyes of his heart recognised God; this squares, in my opinion, with what we have found in Civ 16).

To summarise, we may highlight a number of trends in the use of the Sodom and Gomorrah tradition in the writings of the early Christian Fathers:

1. In principle Sodom remains a symbol of wickedness and punishment, but the emphasis is on other, more specific motifs.

2. The Sodomite sin is seen as allegiance to other gods (Clement of Rome), atheism (Clement of Alexandria), and used in arguments against the gods (Tertullian).

3. The Sodom theme is sometimes associated with that of the flood (Tertullian) and with the Watchers/angels (Irenaeus), betraying the influence of an old Jewish tradition which was probably mediated by the New Testament.

4. Most marked is the evidence, found time and again, that the Fathers interpret and use the Sodom and Gomorrah tradition from the vantage point of their specific theological positions. It is often used in support of christological arguments: Christ appeared to Abraham (Novatian, Tertullian, Hilary, and others); Christ (Justin) or the Word (Irenaeus) punished Sodom. Trinitarian views too are supported in this way (Origen, Cyril of Alexandria, Augustine and others). The tradition can be used to undergird Montanist thinking (Tertullian) and to oppose Marcion (Tertullian) or Arianism (Basil). Tertullian uses the tradition with the backing of juridical learning.

5. Several times the wife of Lot is held up as an admonition to Christians not to look back to the sinful lives that lie behind them (Clement of Rome, Jerome, Augustine), but to be alert and look to the future (Irenaeus).

6. The tradition is employed several times in support of ascetic criticism of marriage/sexuality (Tertullian, Jerome) and wine (Jerome). The sin of Sodom is seen as sexual transgressions (Macarius of Egypt) and as homosexuality (Augustine).

5.3. Conclusions

During the period which interests us here the small literary collection of the New Testament was growing into an important document in the Church. Nevertheless, the New Testament use of the Sodom and Gomorrah tradition is not mirrored by what we have found in the vast corpus of the patristic literature. The tradition is read with *Christian* eyes, but this does not mean *New Testament* eyes.

The symbolism of Sodom and Gomorrah as the types of wickedness and God's punishment is still there, as it has been since the earliest times in the traditions underlying the story of Genesis 18-19, the prophets and the other biblical instances of its use, and as it remained through the centuries in the Jewish and New Testament literature. But in the Fathers' thinking this is not emphasised as such. The same goes for the Synoptic use of the tradition to drive home the vital importance of accepting the message of Jesus. Although this is implicitly present in the thinking of the Fathers, they use the Sodom and Gomorrah tradition exclusively in terms of the issues that were topical in their own time. The only motif used by them with the same purpose and impact as in the New Testament (Luke) is the injunction not to hark back to the past.

For the Fathers the tradition affords opportunities to expound their own interpretations of Christianity. Therefore the biblical material is read for the purposes of the theological, philosophical and juridical defence of Christianity. So the issues found by them in the Sodom and Gomorrah traditions relate to the problem of pagan gods, to christology, trinitarianism, and the inner-Christian debates like that caused by Marcion's brand of gnosticism, the Arian controversies and asceticism. These are the aspects of the background against which we should see the early Christian use of the tradition.

Postscript

Throughout this study I have given summaries of chapters and of the major sections within them (in Chapters 3, 4 and 5). The findings to which my investigation has led with respect to what the different traditions looked like – what the dominant motifs in the various stages of the development were and in what relationships these motifs stood to their respective religious and philosophical contexts (cf p 13) – have been set out in these overviews. So there is no need to repeat them in a conventional 'Conclusion'. Rather than provide another summary I propose to take up the hypothesis that I have put forward in the Introduction (p 13) and answer the question what has become of it in the course of the study.

It has been tested and, in my opinion, vindicated by the arguments developed in the preceding chapters.

1. **Genesis 18-19 has indeed proved to form a literary unit**. We have found evidence for this not merely by assuming as our point of departure that the text 'as it is' must be a unity that makes sense (which in itself would be a perfectly legitimate approach), but by subjecting the text 'as it is', its structure, patterns and motifs, to a close reading. This does not by definition *exclude* historical aspects, but serves as a *gateway* to different levels at which the text can be read. Evidence of a finely composed and balanced 'final text' provides no argument against its being a historically stratified text. To take up the metaphor of the Introduction: We have found evidence of arteries flowing underground, earlier traditions lying behind the narrative of Genesis 18-19. The way in which these flowed together in the fountainhead, that is, the way in which the author used these received materials, could be studied in the light of traditions. In other words, we could study our author's reception of earlier material. Admittedly, these traditions have been reconstructed, but that does not make their use illegitimate – just as little as the reconstruction of what lies behind an obvious murder is illegitimate detective practice. What aspect of our knowledge, after all, is *not* (re)construction? We have, along this way, found that our author was a receiver of traditions and an effective one at that. For he created a narrative which many others would for centuries be glad to receive as well and in their turn again build into creations of their own. This brings us to the second part of our hypothesis:

139

2. The narrative of Genesis 18-19 indeed inspired a rich tradition. Although some Old Testament texts testify to other authors who received the Sodom and Gomorrah traditions in the same way as the author of the Sodom Cycle, the latter became the inspirer *par excellence* of the following generations. His work became the fountainhead from which a tradition stream gushed forth which was to irrigate many greatly differing perspectives. From Ezekiel to Ben Sira, from the Testaments to Josephus, from Philo to the rabbis, from the Synoptics to the late books of the New Testament, from Montanists to Augustine – all stand down-stream in the same river that appeared above ground at Genesis 18-19. The meaning which the Sodom and Gomorrah tradition had for these users differed continuously, but there are also similarities among them. Their own impact varied greatly. Some had limited influence, others cumulatively influenced both Oriental and Western thinking by handing down their own experience of the tradition. Probably the main shift in the meaning of the tradition should be ascribed to the immense influence of Augustine, so that the important social aspect of the Sodom and Gomorrah theme was superseded by the sexual aspect, resulting in the creation of common words as 'sodomy' in which only the sexual aspect of the tradition is remembered.

All the contributors to the perpetuating of the tradition are united in that they share a common heritage. But their varying religious, philosophical, theological and historical backgrounds made varying demands upon their abilities to use the heritage. For this very purpose, however, these settings within which they worked also provided them with the interpretative perspectives on the tradition. That is how the reception and re-creation of traditions work. That is how they are kept alive.

Works Consulted

Albrektson, B. *et al* , 1981, *Remembering all the way... A collection of Old Testament essays published on occasion of the fortieth anniversary of the Oudtestamentisch Werkgezelschap in Nederland*, Leiden: Brill (OTS 21).

Albright, W.F., 1955, Palestinian inscriptions, In Pritchard (ed) 1955:320-322.

Altaner, B. & Stuiber, A., 1966, *Patrologie. Leben, Schriften und Lehre der Kirchenväter*, 7. Aufl., Freiburg: Herder.

Amsler, S., 1965, In Jacob, Keller & Amsler 1965.

Bacher, W., [1892] 1965, *Die Agada der palästinensischen Amoräer*, Bd 1. Hildesheim: Olms, Bd 2: [1896] 1965, Bd 3: [1899] 1965.

–, [1913] 1967, *Die Agada der babylonischen Amoräer*, Hildesheim: Olms.

Baltzer, K., 1964, *Das Bundesformular*, 2. Aufl., Neukirchen: Neukirchener Verlag (WMANT 4).

Barr, J., 1968, The image of God in the Book of Genesis - a study of terminology, *BJRL* 51,11-26.

Bartels, K. & Huber, L. (eds), 1965, *Lexikon der Alten Welt*, Zürich: Artemis.

Bauckham, R.J., 1983, *Jude, 2 Peter*, Waco: Word Books, (Word Biblical Commentary 50).

Berger, K., 1970, Hartherzigkeit und Gottes Gesetz. Die Vorgeschichte des antijüdischen Vorwurfs in Mc 10:5, *ZNW* 61,1-47.

Bonsirven, J., 1953, *La Bible Apocryphe en marge de l'Ancien Testament*, Paris: Fayard.

Bowker, J., 1969, *The targums and Rabbinic literature. An introduction to Jewish interpretations of Scripture*, Cambridge: CUP.

Brockington, L.H., 1961, *A critical introduction to the Apocrypha*, London: Duckworth.

Brownlee, W.H., 1986, *Ezekiel 1-19*, Waco: Word Books (Word Biblical Commentary 28).

Brueggemann, W., 1965, Amos 4 and Israel's covenant worship, *VT* 15,1-15.

–, 1982, *Genesis*, Atlanta: John Knox Press (Interpretation).

Carroll, R.P., 1986, *Jeremiah. A commentary*, London: SCM (OTL).

Charles, R.H., 1895, *maṣḥafa kufâlê* or *The Ethiopic version of the Hebrew Book of Jubilees*, Oxford: Clarendon (Anecdota Oxoniensa).

Clapp, F.G., 1936, The site of Sodom and Gomorrah, *American Journal of Archaeology* 40,323-344.

Colson, F.H. & Whitaker, G.H., [1929] 1971, *Philo*, Vol 1, London: Heinemann, (LCL); Vol 2: [1927] 1979; Vol 3: [1930] 1954; Vol 4: [1932] 1968; Vol 5: [1934] 1968; Vol 6: [1935] 1966 (Colson only).

Colpe, C., 1961, Philo, *RGG*, 3. Aufl., Bd. 5,341-346.

Crenshaw, J.L., 1970, Popular questioning of the justice of God in Ancient Israel, *ZAW* 82,380-395.

Dancy, J.C., 1972, *The shorter books of the Apocrypha. Tobit, Judith, Rest of Esther, Baruch, Letter of Jeremiah, Additions to Daniel and Prayer of Manasseh*, Cambridge: CUP, (CBC).

Delitzsch, F., 1888-9, *A new commentary on Genesis*, Edinburgh: T & T Clark (tr by S. Taylor).

Denis, A-M., 1970, *Introduction aux Pseudépigraphes Grecs d'Ancien Testament*, Leiden: Brill, (Studia in Veteris Testamenti Pseudepigrapha 1).

Dentan, R.C., 1963, The literary affinities of Exodus 34:6f, *VT* 13,34-51.

Descamps, A. & Halleux, R.P.A. de, 1970, *Melanges bibliques en hommage au R P Béda Rigaux*, Gembloux: Duculot.

Dillmann, A., 1892, *Die Genesis*, 6. Aufl., Leipzig: Hirzel, (KeHAT).

Donner, H., 1963, Kallirrhoë. Das Sanatorium Herodes' des Grossen, *ZDPV* 79,59-89.

Driver, S.R., [1902] 1960, *A critical and exegetical commentary on Deuteronomy*, 3rd ed, Edinburgh: T & T Clark, (ICC).

Duhm, B., 1902, *Das Buch Jesaia*, 2. Aufl., Göttingen: Vandenhoeck & Ruprecht, (GHKAT).

Eissfeldt, O., 1962, Sodom und Gomorrha, *RGG*, 3. Aufl., Bd. 6,114-115.

–, 1965, *The Old Testament. An Introduction including the Apocrypha and Pseudepigrapha, and also the works of similar type from Qumran*, Oxford: Blackwell.

Emerton, J.A., 1971a, Some false clues in the study of Genesis 14, *VT* 21,24-47.

–, 1971b, The riddle of Genesis 14, *VT* 21,403-439.

Fitzmyer, J.A., 1985, *The Gospel according to Luke (10-24). Introduction, translation, and notes*, Garden City: Doubleday, (AB).

Foerster, W., 1959, Josephus, *RGG*, 3. Aufl., Bd. 3,868-869.

Fohrer, G., 1955, *Ezechiel*, Tübingen: J.C.B. Mohr, (HAT 13).

–, 1965, *Einleitung in das Alte Testament*, 10. Aufl., Heidelberg: Quelle & Meyer.

Franxman, Th.W., 1979, *Genesis and the 'Jewish Antiquities' of Flavius Josephus*, Rome: Biblical Institute Press, (Biblica et Orientalia 35).

Freedman, H., 1951, *Midrash Rabbah. Genesis*, 2 vols, London: Soncino.

Fripp, E.I., 1892, Note on Genesis 18.19, *ZAW* 12,23-29.

Gaster, T.H., 1969, *Myth, legend and custom in the Old Testament. A comparative study with chapters from Sir James G. Frazer's 'Folklore in the Old Testament'*, New York: Harper & Row.

Gese, H., 1962, Weisheit, *RGG*, 3. Aufl., Bd. 6,1574-1577.

Gesenius, W., See Kautzsch, E.

Gibert, P., 1974, Légende ou saga? *VT* 24,411-420.

Ginsberg, H.L., 1951, A preposition of interest to historical geographers, *BASOR* 122,12-14.

Ginzberg, L., 1900, *Die Haggada bei den Kirchenvätern und in der apokryphischen Litteratur*, Berlin: Calvary.

–, 1909-1938, *The legends of the Jews*, Philadelphia: The Jewish Publication Society of America; Vol 1: 1909; Vol 2: 1910; Vol 3: 1911; Vol 4: 1913; Vol 5: 1925; Vol 6: 1928; Vol 7: 1938 (by Cohen, B.).

Gitay, Y., 1984, Review of Rudin-O'Brasky 1982, *JBL* 103,639-640.

Gnilka, J., 1986, *Das Matthäusevangelium. 1. Teil. Kommentar zu Kap 1:1 - 13:58*, Freiburg: Herder, (Herders theologischer Kommentar zum Neuen Testament).

Goetze, A., 1955, Hittite treaties, In Pritchard (ed) 1955:201-206.

Goodenough, E.R., 1962, *An introduction to Philo Judaeus*, 2nd ed, Oxford: Blackwell.

Gottwald, N.K., 1962, *Studies in the Book of Lamentations*, 2nd ed, London: SCM, (SBT).

Grundmann, W., 1974, *Der Brief des Judas und der zweite Brief des Petrus*, Berlin: Evangelische Verlagsanstalt, (ThHNT 15).

Gunkel, H., 1910, *Genesis*, 3. Aufl., Göttingen: Vandenhoeck & Ruprecht, (GHKAT).

Hagner, D.A., 1973, *The use of the Old and New Testaments in Clement of Rome*, Leiden: Brill, (SNT 34).

Harland, J.P., 1942-3, Sodom and Gomorrah, *BA* 5/2,17-32, 6/3,41-54.

Hattem, W.C. van, 1981, Once again: Sodom and Gomorrah, *BA* 44,87-92.

Heinemann, I., [1929-1932] 1962, *Philons griechische und jüdische Bildung. Kulturvergleichende untersuchungen zu Philons Darstellung der jüdischen Gesetze*, Hildesheim: Olms.

Herford, R.T., [1933] 1971, *Talmud and Apocrypha. A comparative study of the Jewish ethical teaching in the Rabbinical and non-Rabbinical sources in the early centuries*, New York: Ktav.

Hillers, D.R., 1964, *Treaty curses and the Old Testament prophets*, Rome: Pontifical Biblical Institute, (Biblica et Orientalia).

Holladay, W.L., 1986, *A commentary on the Book of the Prophet Jeremiah Chapters 1-25*, Philadelphia: Fortress, (Hermeneia).

Hollander, H.W. & De Jonge, M., 1985, *The Testaments of the Twelve Patriarchs. A commentary*, Leiden: Brill, (Studia in Veteris Testamenti Pseudepigrapha 8).

Horst, F., See Robinson, T.H. & Horst, F.

Jacob, B., [1934] 1974, *Genesis*, New York: Ktav.

Jacob, E.; Keller, C-A. & Amsler, S., 1965, *Osée - Joël - Abdias - Jonas - Amos*, Neuchâtel: Delachaux & Niestlé, (Commentaire de l'Ancien Testament 11a).

Jepsen, A., 1953-4, Zur Ueberlieferungsgeschichte der Vätergestalten, *Wissenschaftliche Zeitschrift der Karl-Marx-Universität*, Gesellschafts- und Sprachwissenschaftliche Reihe 2/3.

Jolles, A., 1930, *Einfache Formen. Legende, Sage, Mythe, Rätsel, Spruch, Kasus, Memorabile, Märchen, Witz*, Tübingen: Max Niemeyer.

Jonge, M. de, 1979, The interpretation of the Twelve Patriarchs in recent years, In De Jonge (ed) 1979:183-192.

Jonge, M. de (ed), 1975, *Studies on the Testaments of the Twelve Patriarchs. Text and interpretation*, Leiden: Brill, (Studia in Veteris Testamenti Pseudepigrapha 3).

Jonge, M. de, 1985, See Hollander & De Jonge 1985.

Kaiser, O., 1981, *Das Buch des Propheten Jesaja, kapitel 1-12*, Göttingen: Vandenhoeck & Ruprecht, (ATD 17).

Kautzsch, E., [1910] 1966, *Gesenius' Hebrew Grammar*, 2nd English ed in accordance with the 28th German ed, tr by A.E. Cowley, Oxford: Clarendon.

Keel, O., 1979, Wer zerstörte Sodom? *Th Z* 35,10-17.

Kilian, R., 1966, *Die vorpriesterlichen Abrahamsüberlieferungen, literarkritisch und traditionsgeschichtlich untersucht*, Bonn: Hanstein, (BBB).

–, 1970, Zur Ueberlieferungsgeschichte Lots, *BZ* NF 14,23-37.

Klein, F.N., 1962, *Die Lichtterminologie bei Philon von Alexandrien und in den hermetischen Schriften. Untersuchungen zur Struktur der religiösen Sprache der hellenistischen Mystik*, Leiden: Brill.

Klostermann, E., 1966, *Eusebius. Das Onomastikon der biblischen Ortsnamen*, Hildesheim: Olms.

Koester, H., 1968, *Nomos phuseós*, The concept of natural law in Greek thought, In Neusner (ed) 1968:521-541.

Kraetschmar, R., 1897, Der Mythus von Sodoms Ende, *ZAW* 17,81-92.

Kraus, H.J., 1968, *Klagelieder (Threni)*, 2. Aufl., Neukirchen: Neukirchener Verlag, (BK 20).

Lagrange, M.J., 1932, Le site du Sodome d'apres les textes, *RB* 41,489-514.

Lamparter, H., 1972a, *Die Apokryphen 1. Das Buch Jesus Sirach*, Stuttgart: Calwer, (BAT 25/1).

–, 1972b, *Die Apokryphen 2. Weisheit Salomos, Tobias, Judith, Baruch*, Stuttgart: Calwer, (BAT 25/2).

Lang, F., 1950, *Das Feuer im Sprachgebrauch der Bibel, dargestellt auf dem Hintergrund der Feuervorstellungen in der Umwelt*, Diss Tübingen.

–, 1959, *pur*, *ThWNT* 6,927-948.

Lasine, S., 1984, Guest and host in Judges 19: Lot's hospitality in an inverted world, *JSOT* 29,37-59.

Lawler, T.C. & Mierow, C.C., 1963, *The letters of Saint Jerome*, 2 vols., London: Longmans.

Lods, A., 1927, La caverne de Lot, *RHR* 95,204-219.

Lohfink, N., 1962, Der Bundesschluss im Land Moab, *BZ* NF 6,32-56.

Lührmann, D., 1969, *Die Redaktion der Logienquelle*, Neukirchen: Neukirchener Verlag, (WMANT 33).

–, 1972, Noah und Lot (Lk 17:26-29) - ein Nachtrag, *ZNW* 63,130-132.

MacDonald, J., 1963, *Memar Marqah. The teaching of Marqah*, 2 vols., Berlin: Töpelmann, (BZAW 84).

Marcus, R., [1953] 1979, *Philo. Supplement 1: Questions and answers on Genesis*, London: Heinemann, (LCL).

Marshall, I.H., 1978, *The Gospel of Luke. A commentary on the Greek text*, Exeter: Paternoster, (The New International Greek Testament Commentary).

Michel, O., 1978, *Der Brief an die Römer*, 14. Aufl., Göttingen: Vandenhoeck & Ruprecht, (KeKNT 4).

Mulder, M.J., 1970, *Het meisje van Sodom*, Inaugural lecture, Free University of Amsterdam, Kampen: Kok.

Neher, A., 1979, Ezechiel, rédempteur de Sodome, *RHPR* 59,483-490.

Neusner, J. (ed), 1968, *Religions in Antiquity. Essays in memory of E.R. Goodenough*, Leiden: Brill.

Noth, M., 1948, *Ueberlieferungsgeschichte des Pentateuchs*, Stuttgart: Kohlhammer.

Oppenheim, A.L., 1955, Babylonian and Assyrian historical texts. In Pritchard (ed) 1955:265-315.

Perlitt, L., 1969, *Bundestheologie im Alten Testament*, Neukirchen: Neukirchener Verlag, (WMANT 36).

Plöger, O., 1969, *Die Klagelieder*, Tübingen: J.C.B. Mohr, (In HAT 18: *Die fünf Megillot*).

Preuss, H.D., 1982, *Deuteronomium*, Darmstadt: WBG, (Erträge der Forschung 164).

Pritchard, J.B. (ed), 1955, *Ancient Near Eastern Texts relating to the Old Testament*, 2nd ed., Princeton: Princeton University Press.

Procksch, O., 1906, *Die Elohimquelle*, Leipzig: Hinrichs.

–, 1913, *Die Genesis*, Leipzig: Deichert, (KAT 1).

Rad, G. von, 1964a, *Das erste Buch Mose. Genesis*, Göttingen: Vandenhoeck & Ruprecht, (ATD 2-4).

–, 1964b, *Das fünfte Buch Mose. Deuteronomium*, Göttingen: Vandenhoeck & Ruprecht, (ATD 8).

Rengstorff, K.H., 1958, *Das Evangelium nach Lukas*, 8. Aufl., Göttingen: Vandenhoeck & Ruprecht, (NTD 3).

Riessler, P., 1928, *Altjüdisches Schrifttum ausserhalb der Bibel*, Heidelberg: Kerle.

Robinson, T.H. & Horst, F., 1964, *Die zwölf kleinen Propheten*, 3. Aufl., Tübingen: J.C.B. Mohr, (HAT 14).

Rost, L., 1971, *Einleitung in die alttestamentlichen Apokryphen und Pseudepigraphen einschliesslich der grossen Qumran-Handschriften*, Heidelberg: Quelle & Meyer.

Rudin-O'Brasky, T., 1982, *The patriarchs in Hebron and Sodom (Genesis 18-19). A study of the structure and composition of a biblical story*, Jerusalem: Simor, (Jerusalem Biblical Studies 2), In Hebrew.

Rudolph, W., 1958, *Jeremiah*, 2 Aufl., Tübingen: J.C.B. Mohr, (HAT 12).

–, 1966, *Hosea*, Gütersloh, Gerd Mohn, (KAT 13/1).

–, 1971, *Joel - Amos - Obadja - Jona*, Gütersloh: Gerd Mohn, (KAT 13/2).

Sabottka, L., 1972, *Zephanja. Versuch einer Neuübersetzung mit philologischem Kommentar*, Rome: Pontificium Institutum Biblicum, (Biblica et Orientalia 25).

Scharbert, J., 1986, *Genesis 12-50*, Würzburg: Echter Verlag, (Die Neue Echter Bibel).

Schatz, W., 1972, Genesis 14: Eine Untersuchung, *Europäische Hochschulschrift* 23/2,175-181.

Schlosser, J., 1973, Les jours de Noé et de Lot. A propos de Luc 17:26-30, *RB* 80,13-36.

Schmid, H.H., 1966, *Wesen und Geschichte der Weisheit*, Berlin: Töpelmann, (BZAW 101).

–, 1976, *Der sogenannte Jahwist. Beobachtungen und Fragen zur Pentateuchforschung*, Zürich: Theologischer Verlag.

Schmidt, H.W., 1963, *Der Brief des Paulus an die Römer*, Berlin: Evangelische Verlagsanstalt, (ThHNT 6).

Schmidt, L., 1976, *'De Deo'. Studien zur Literarkritik und Theologie des Buches Jona, des Gespräches zwischen Abraham und Jahwe in Gen 18:22ff und von Hi 1*, Berlin: De Gruyter, (BZAW 143).

Schnackenburg, R., 1970, Der eschatologische Abschnitt Lk 17:20-37, In Descamps & De Halleux 1970:213-234.

Schürer, E., s. a. [=1909]. *A history of the Jewish People in the time of Jesus Christ*, 5 vols (a-e) in 2 divisions, New York: Scribner, (German original 1901-1909).

Selms, A. van, 1967, *Genesis. Deel 1*, Nijkerk: Callenbach, (POT).

Seters, J. van, 1975, *Abraham in history and tradition*, New Haven: Yale University Press.

Shafer, B.E., 1984, Review of Rudin-O'Brasky 1982, *CBQ* 46,772-773.

Shutt, R.J.H., 1961, *Studies in Josephus*, London: SPCK.

Simons, J., 1948, Two notes on the problem of the Pentapolis, *OTS* 5,91-117.

Skinner, J., 1930, *A critical and exegetical commentary on Genesis*, 2nd ed, Edinburgh: T & T Clark, (ICC).

Smith, J.P., 1952, *St Irenaeus. Proof of the Apostolic preaching*, London: Longmans & Green, (Ancient Christian Writers 16).

Stolz, F., 1976, *ns'*, *THAT* 2,109-117.

Speiser, E.A., 1964, *Genesis. Introduction, translation and notes*, 2nd ed, Garden City: Doubleday, (AB).

Spicq, C., 1966, *Les épitres de Saint Pierre*, Paris: Gabalda, (SB).

Strack, H.L., [1931] 1969, *Introduction to the Talmud and Midrash*, New York: Atheneum.

– & Billerbeck, P., [1922-1926] 1965, *Kommentar zum Neuen Testament aus Talmud und Midrasch*, 4. Aufl., München: Beck.

Thackeray, H.St.J., [1928] 1957, *Josephus*, Vol 3, *The Jewish War, Books 4-7*, London: Heinemann, (LCL).

–, [1930] 1961, *Josephus*, Vol 4, *Jewish Antiquities, Books 1-4*, London: Heinemann, (LCL).

– & Marcus, R., [1934] 1958, *Josephus*, Vol 5, *Jewish Antiquities, Books 5-8*, London: Heinemann, (LCL).

Thunberg, L., 1966, Early Christian interpretations of the three angels in Gn 18, *Stud Patr* 7/1,560-570.

Thyen, H., 1965, Philon von Alexandrien, *LAW*, 2301-2302.

Uchelen, N.A. van, 1981, Isaiah 1:9: Text and context, In Albrektson *et al* (ed) 1981:155-163.

VanderKam, J.C., 1977, *Textual and historical studies in the Book of Jubilees*, Missoula: Scholars, (Harvard Semitic Monographs).

Varneda, V.I., 1986, *The historical method of Flavius Josephus*, Leiden: Brill, (ALGHJ 19).

Vawter, B., 1977, *On Genesis: A new reading*, Garden City: Doubleday.

Volz, P., 1934, *Die Eschatologie der jüdischen Gemeinde im neutesta-*

mentlichen Zeitalter nach den Quellen der rabbinischen, apokalyptischen und apokryphen Literatur, Tübingen: Mohr.

Wahl, O., 1977, *Apocalypsis Esdrae. Apocalypsis Sedrach. Visio Beati Esdrae*, Leiden: Brill, (Pseudepigrapha Veteris Testamenti Graece 4).

Watts, J.D.W., 1985, *Isaiah 1-33*, Waco: Word Books, (Word Biblical Commentary 24).

Wallis, G., 1966, Die Stadt in den Ueberlieferungen der Genesis, *ZAW* 78,133-148.

–, 1969, Die Tradition von den drei Ahnvätern, *ZAW* 81,18-40.

Weinfeld, M., 1972, *Deuteronomy and the Deuteronomic School*, Oxford: Clarendon.

Weiser, A., 1962, *Klagelieder*, Göttingen: Vandenhoeck & Ruprecht, (ATD 16).

–, 1966, *Einleitung in das Alte Testament*, 6. Aufl., Göttingen: Vandenhoeck & Ruprecht.

Wellhausen, J., 1889, *Die Composition des Hexateuchs und der historischen Bücher des Alten Testaments*, 2. Aufl., Berlin: G. Reimer.

Westermann, C., 1976a, *Die Verheissungen an die Väter. Studien zur Vätergeschichte*, Göttingen: Vandenhoeck & Ruprecht.

–, 1976b, *Genesis. 1. Teilband, Genesis 1-11*, 2. Aufl., Neukirchen: Neukirchener Verlag, (BK 1/1).

–, 1981, *Genesis. 2. Teilband, Genesis 12-36*, Neukirchen: Neukirchener Verlag, (BK 1/2).

Wevers, J.W., 1969, *Ezekiel*, London: Nelson, (CB).

Wilckens, U., 1980, *Der Brief an die Römer*, 3 Bde., Neukirchen: Neukirchener Verlag, (EKK 6).

Wildberger, H., 1972, *Jesaja. 1. Teilband, Jesaja 1-12*, Neukirchen: Neukirchener Verlag, (BK 10/1).

Williamson, R., 1970, *Philo and the Epistle to the Hebrews*, Leiden: Brill, (ALGHJ 4).

Winston, D., 1982, *The Wisdom of Solomon. A new translation and commentary*, Garden City: Doubleday, (AB).

Wolff, H.W., 1965, *Dodekapropheton 1. Hosea*, 2. Aufl., Neukirchen: Neukirchener Verlag, (BK 14/1).

–, 1969, *Dodekapropheton 2. Joel und Amos*, Neukirchen: Neukirchener Verlag, (BK 14/2).

Zimmerli, W., 1969, *Ezechiel. 1. Teilband, Ezechiel 1-24*, Neukirchen: Neukirchener Verlag, (BK 13/1).

–, 1976, *1 Mose 12-25*, Zürich: Theologischer Verlag, (ZB).

Zmijewski, J., 1972, *Die Eschatologiereden des Lukasevangeliums. Eine traditions- und redaktionsgeschichtliche Untersuchung zu Lk 21:5-36 und Lk 17:20-37*, Bonn: Hanstein, (BBB 40).

List of Abbreviations

AB	The Anchor Bible.
ALGHJ	Arbeiten zur Literatur und Geschichte des hellenistischen Judentums.
ATD	Das Alte Testament Deutsch.
BA	The Biblical Archaeologist.
BASOR	Bulletin of the American Schools of Oriental Research.
BAT	Die Botschaft des Alten Testaments.
BBB	Bonner biblische Beiträge.
BJRL	Bulletin of the John Rylands Library.
BK	Biblischer Kommentar.
BZ	Biblische Zeitschrift.
BZAW	Beihefte zur Zeitschrift für die alttestamentliche Wissenschaft.
CB	The Clarendon Bible.
CBC	The Cambridge Bible Commentary.
CBQ	Catholic Biblical Quarterly.
EKK	Evangelisch-katholische Kommentar zum Neuen Testament.
GHKAT	Göttinger Handkommentar zum Alten Testament.
HAT	Handbuch zum Alten Testament.
ICC	The International Critical Commentary.
JBL	Journal of Biblical Literature.
JSOT	Journal for the Study of the Old Testament.
KAT	Kommentar zum Alten Testament.
KeHAT	Kurzgefasstes exegetisches Handbuch zum Alten Testament.
KeKNT	Kritisch-exegetischer Kommentar über das Neue Testament.
LAW	Lexikon der Alten Welt.
LCL	Loeb Classical Library.
NTD	Das Neue Testament Deutsch.
OTL	Old Testament Library.
OTS	Oudtestamentische Studiën.
PG	Migne, J.P., 1857-1866. *Patrologiae cursus completus. Series Graeca*, Turnholt: Brepols.
PL	Migne, J.P., 1844-1864. *Patrologiae cursus completus. Series Latina*, Paris: L. Migne.
POT	De Prediking van het Oude Testament.
RB	Revue Biblique.

RGG   Galling, K. (ed), 1957-1965, *Die Religion in Geschichte und Gegenwart*, 3. Aufl., Tübingen: J.C.B. Mohr.
RHPR Revue d'Histoire et de Philosophie Religieuses.
RHR   Revue de l'Histoire des Religions.
SNT   Supplements to Novum Testamentum.
SB   Sources Bibliques.
SBT   Studies in Biblical Theology.
Stud Patr Studia Patristica.
THAT Jenni, E. & Westermann, C. (eds), 1971-1976, *Theologisches Handwörterbuch zum Alten Testament*, 2 Bde., München: Kaiser.
ThHNT Theologischer Handkommentar zum Neuen Testament.
ThWNT Kittel, G. & Friedrich, G. (eds), 1933-1979, *Theologisches Wörterbuch zum Neuen Testament*, Stuttgart: Kohlhammer.
ThZ   Theologische Zeitschrift.
WMANT Wissenschaftliche Monographien zum Alten und Neuen Testament.
VT   Vetus Testamentum.
ZAW   Zeitschrift für die alttestamentliche Wissenschaft.
ZB   Zürcher Bibelkommentare.
ZDPV Zeitschrift des deutschen Palästinavereins.
ZNW   Zeitschrift für die neutestamentliche Wissenschaft.

DATE DUE

DEC 19 1993			
			\